Six Lost Years

THE AZRIELI SERIES OF HOLOCAUST SURVIVOR MEMOIRS: PUBLISHED TITLES

Six Lost Years
Amek Adler

THE AZRIELI FOUNDATION
www.azrielifoundation.org

Cover and book design by Mark Goldstein
Endpaper maps by Martin Gilbert
Map on page xxxi by François Blanc

LIBRARY AND ARCHIVES CANADA CATALOGUING IN PUBLICATION

Amek, author
    Six lost years / Amek Adler.

(Azrieli series of Holocaust survivor memoirs. Series IX)
Includes index.
ISBN 978-1-988065-18-2 (softcover)

1. Adler, Amek. 2. Holocaust survivors — Poland — Biography. 3. Holocaust survivors — Canada — Biography. 4. Holocaust, Jewish (1939–1945) — Poland — Personal narratives. I. Azrieli Foundation, issuing body. II. Title.

DS134.72.A35A3 2017   940.53'18092   C2017-900895-1

PRINTED IN CANADA

The Azrieli Series of Holocaust Survivor Memoirs

Naomi Azrieli, Publisher

Jody Spiegel, Program Director
Arielle Berger, Managing Editor
Farla Klaiman, Editor
Matt Carrington, Editor
Elizabeth Lasserre, Senior Editor, French-Language Editions
Elin Beaumont, Senior Education Outreach and Program Facilitator
Catherine Person, Educational Outreach and Events Coordinator,
    Quebec and French Canada
Marc-Olivier Cloutier, Educational Outreach and Events Assistant,
    Quebec and French Canada
Tim MacKay, Digital Platform Manager
Elizabeth Banks, Digital Asset Curator and Archivist
Susan Roitman, Office Manager (Toronto)
Mary Mellas, Executive Assistant and Human Resources (Montreal)

Mark Goldstein, Art Director
François Blanc, Cartographer
Bruno Paradis, Layout, French-Language Editions

Contents

Series Preface:
In their own words...

In telling these stories, the writers have liberated themselves. For so many years we did not speak about it, even when we became free people living in a free society. Now, when at last we are writing about what happened to us in this dark period of history, knowing that our stories will be read and live on, it is possible for us to feel truly free. These unique historical documents put a face on what was lost, and allow readers to grasp the enormity of what happened to six million Jews — one story at a time.

David J. Azrieli, C.M., C.Q., M.Arch
Holocaust survivor and founder, The Azrieli Foundation

Since the end of World War II, over 30,000 Jewish Holocaust survivors have immigrated to Canada. Who they are, where they came from, what they experienced and how they built new lives for themselves and their families are important parts of our Canadian heritage. The Azrieli Foundation's Holocaust Survivor Memoirs Program was established to preserve and share the memoirs written by those who survived the twentieth-century Nazi genocide of the Jews of Europe and later made their way to Canada. The program is guided by the conviction that each survivor of the Holocaust has a remarkable story to tell, and that such stories play an important role in education about tolerance and diversity.

Millions of individual stories are lost to us forever. By preserving the stories written by survivors and making them widely available to a broad audience, the Azrieli Foundation's Holocaust Survivor Memoirs Program seeks to sustain the memory of all those who perished at the hands of hatred, abetted by indifference and apathy. The personal accounts of those who survived against all odds are as different as the people who wrote them, but all demonstrate the courage, strength, wit and luck that it took to prevail and survive in such terrible adversity. The memoirs are also moving tributes to people — strangers and friends — who risked their lives to help others, and who, through acts of kindness and decency in the darkest of moments, frequently helped the persecuted maintain faith in humanity and courage to endure. These accounts offer inspiration to all, as does the survivors' desire to share their experiences so that new generations can learn from them.

The Holocaust Survivor Memoirs Program collects, archives and publishes these distinctive records and the print editions are available free of charge to educational institutions and Holocaust-education programs across Canada. They are also available for sale to the general public at bookstores. All revenues to the Azrieli Foundation from the sales of the Azrieli Series of Holocaust Survivor Memoirs go toward the publishing and educational work of the memoirs program.

The Azrieli Foundation would like to express appreciation to the following people for their invaluable efforts in producing this book: Doris Bergen, Ron Csillag, Sherry Dodson (Maracle Press), Barbara Kamieński, Therese Parent, and Margie Wolfe & Emma Rodgers of Second Story Press.

About the Glossary

The following memoir contains a number of terms, concepts and historical references that may be unfamiliar to the reader. For information on major organizations; significant historical events and people; geographical locations; religious and cultural terms; and foreign-language words and expressions that will help give context and background to the events described in the text, please see the glossary beginning on page 71.

Introduction

Amek Adler lived in Lodz with his grandmother, parents and three brothers when World War II broke out on September 1, 1939. As the war continued and Nazi persecution intensified, Amek moved from place to place. Each move included fewer family members. Although some of his close relatives did survive, Amek was liberated near the Austrian border without any of his family. Being subjected to multiple transfers and types of living conditions (ghettos, labour camps and concentration camps) and gradually being separated from family members were typical experiences for Jews who survived the Holocaust through labour. Because of their war needs, the Nazis temporarily allowed some "work Jews" to live until they found replacement workers.[1] Meanwhile, they exploited Jewish workers by keeping them in guarded segregated places and transferring them in accordance with war exigencies.

Amek's fate was different from that of most Jewish children his age. The support Amek received from his older brother, Ben, greatly contributed to his survival. Jews who were interned in labour and concentration camps together with family members had a better chance of survival than those who were on their own. Family members shared extra food they acquired and gave moral support to each other. Ben was Amek's bulwark, finding him work and sharing with him the extra food he received as a payment from Ukrainian and

Nazi guards when he fixed their watches on Sundays in Radom and Vaihingen. Most importantly, Ben saved many family members when the Radom ghettos were liquidated in August 1942. This was exceptional. As Amek describes, the Nazis made a selection in the ghetto's central square to determine who would be transported to Treblinka. After examining work cards, they kept some workers but did not spare their family members. Those who did not have a card were sent immediately to the line that led to the trains. Even holding a card did not guarantee forestallment of deportation. The Nazis mainly kept workers vital for the war industry. They separated family members, retaining the strongest and deporting the oldest and the youngest, which is why Ben's success in hindering the deportation of his parents, wife and two brothers was unique.

The Adler family had moved to Lodz because of the father's occupation in the textile industry. Lodz's prosperous economy was based on this industry, which made Lodz the biggest industrial centre in Poland. The German air force bombed the city several times during the first week of September 1939. Several hundred residents were killed, and the city was in disarray. When the Polish military started to withdraw, a mass flight of young men — many Jews among them — began. In many Polish cities and towns, young Jewish men fled east, fearing that the Germans would send them to labour camps. Their families often stayed behind. During these first three days, about 60,000 people left Lodz. Several thousand among them went to Warsaw following an official broadcast on Polish radio calling for young men to escape there in order to help the Polish military defend the capital.[2] Amek's brother, Ben, was one of them.

During the first month and a half of its occupation, Lodz was under the jurisdiction of the military, whose first order, issued on the eve of the Jewish High Holidays, forbade the Jews to pray in public. The order forced the Jews to close the synagogues and to open their businesses on Saturdays (the Jewish Sabbath) and on Jewish holidays. Two months later, the Germans set fire to and destroyed the three most magnificent synagogues in town. Amek witnessed the burning of one of them, the old synagogue near his home where his family used to pray.

Further persecutions were mainly economic. Anti-Jewish legislation aimed to remove the Jews from the local economy and transfer their businesses to Aryan hands. In that vein, the Germans limited the ways in which Jews could keep and use capital. The Germans blocked all Jewish bank accounts, limiting the amount of cash Jews could hold in, and withdraw from, their accounts. They prohibited Jewish trade in textile and leather products and ordered the marking of Jewish businesses and stores. The Germans then barred Jews from owning property, transferring their businesses to trustees.[3]

In addition to official persecution, Jews in Poland suffered from unofficial mistreatment. Press gangs for labour, which started from the first days of occupation, were the most troubling because of the terror they created. Military, police, SS and even individual Germans rounded up from the streets men, women, youth and occasionally children to toil in hard manual jobs they were not used to doing. Like Amek's father, many press-ganged Jews worked for long hours without breaks or food. While some of the tasks, such as carrying heavy rocks from place to place or cleaning streets, were futile, most — such as repairing the damage done during military campaigns or maintaining the local offices of the German authorities — had practical aims. Nevertheless, the Germans regularly added various types of abuse to the already difficult work conditions, instilling a clear sense of humiliation even for work that fulfilled exigent military needs. In addition, the lack of appropriate tools and the constant physical abuse often resulted in injuries. As a result, many Jews avoided the streets, and their livelihoods were curtailed.

Toward the end of October 1939, the Germans divided Poland into three parts. The eastern region was transferred to Soviet control in accordance with the Molotov-Ribbentrop Pact, signed shortly before the war. The central region — the General Government (*Generalgou-*

vernement) — retained the status of occupied territories. The western region, in which Lodz was included, was annexed to the Reich. Following the annexation, Poles and Jews experienced more severe persecutions that were aimed to encourage them to leave the area.

Three types of persecutions, which Amek mentions in his memoir, are noteworthy. The policies of curfew, wearing a yellow badge and confinement to a ghetto were aimed at limiting the movement of Jews and excluding them from Polish society. These persecutions are typical examples of how Nazi policies against the Jews in all occupied territories in Europe were in some aspects uniform, although other elements varied. While one of the first ordinances the Germans issued when they conquered a country was to ban the Jews from leaving their homes during the night, the time span of the curfew differed by location. In Lodz it was from 5:00 p.m. to 8:00 a.m.; in the General Government it lasted from 9:00 p.m. to 5:00 a.m.; and in Germany the curfew, which was issued when the war broke out in September 1939, was in order between 8:00 p.m. and 6:00 a.m. (9:00 p.m. to 5:00 a.m. in the summer).

The yellow cloth Star of David became one of the most well-known Holocaust symbols. While the Nazis named it the "Jewish Star" (*Judenstern*), the Jews adopted the term "Yellow Badge." Robert Weltsch coined the term in an article he published in April 1933 in the Jewish German newspaper *Jüdische Rundschau* (Jewish Review) following the Nazi boycott of Jewish stores in Germany. The storefronts were identified with a Star of David, apparently reminding Weltsch of the yellow mark Jews had to wear in the Middle Ages. He titled his article: "Bear it with pride, the yellow badge." Even so, in Germany the Jews had to wear the yellow badge "only" from September 1941. The Polish Jews had to wear it beginning in November 1939. The badge worn in the Polish annexed territories was different from that used in the General Government. In Lodz, as in western and central Europe, it was a fist-sized Star of David made out of yellow cloth, with the word "Jude" (Jew) written on it in black. Jews had to wear two badges on their outer clothing, one on the left side of the chest and one on the back. In the General Government, Jews had to wear on their arms a white band with a blue Star of David. In Germany the order was issued to all Jews over six years old, and in the General Government it encompassed all Jews over ten years of age.[4] Amek thus wore both identification badges — in Lodz the yellow badge, and in Warsaw and Radom the blue-and-white band.

Amek had another unusual experience. In three places — Lodz, Warsaw and Radom — he witnessed how a ghetto was constructed, curtailing the living space of the Jews. The Germans did not have an organized and systematic plan for setting up the ghettos. There were ghettos in many places in Poland and the Soviet Union, but not in Western Europe. Those in Poland were set up mostly between October 1939 and December 1941. Some of the ghettos, like those in Lodz, Warsaw and Radom, were closed, with a wall or a fence barring the Jews from leaving; others, like Lublin, were open ghettos, but the Jews were forbidden to leave their neighbourhoods. The first ghetto was established in the small town of Piotrków Trybunalski in central Poland. Established in the spring of 1940, the Lodz ghetto was the first to be set up in a large city.[5] Like other ghettos it was located in poor neighbourhoods. The official German reason for isolating the Jewish population was that they allegedly carried diseases. Thus, Jewish segregation was supposed to control the spread of epidemics. However, the ghettoization was based on practical reasons that interlinked with Nazi ideology regarding the inferiority of the Jewish race. In Lodz, the practical reason for the ghetto was the inability to expel the Jews in a short time, and so the ghetto was supposed to be temporary. In Radom, ghettoization was aimed at transferring Jewish living quarters to the many Germans in town.

During most of the war Amek was in Radom, a city in central Poland, which was the headquarters of the Radom district. The district was one of the original four districts: Krakow, Warsaw, Lublin, and Radom, which comprised the General Government (a fifth district, Galicia, was added following the attack on the Soviet Union in the summer of 1941). In the late nineteenth century, the city became an important industrial centre for leather processing. Samuel Adler, apparently one of Amek's ancestors, was one of the first important entrepreneurs, developing the industry.[6] Thus, Amek's claim that the family belonged to the Jewish aristocracy in Radom had historical roots. The 30,000 Jews who lived in Radom on the eve of World War II, comprising some 30 per cent of its population, were the city's economic backbone; they owned most of the small industries for which it was known: the leather factories, tanneries, iron foundries and lumber mills, as well as the furniture, shoe, enamel, paint and brick factories. In addition, they handled the majority of its commerce. Nevertheless, most Jews worked as artisans.

For the Germans, the city had two main economic advantages, which they exploited for their military needs: it was one of the three most important industrial areas in pre-war Poland, and it stood at the intersection of railroads. When the war expanded eastward in the summer of 1941, the city acquired further important economic and strategic value. The German occupiers established airstrips and transit bases for soldiers, transferred supplies to the front and increased the industrial production of military equipment. These developments had two significant effects on the city's Jews. On the one hand they had to move to a ghetto and live in a very crammed space; on the other hand they had work opportunities, which most Jews in big- and medium-sized ghettos did not have.

Ghettoization in Radom occurred relatively late, in April 1941. Until then local Jews were able to bribe the district governor, Karl Lasch, and thus postpone the establishment of the ghetto. But when military troops arrived in the city as part of the preparations for Operation Barbarossa (the attack on the Soviet Union), the housing shortage became acute. Ghettoization was a means to alleviate the housing deficiency. The many Germans in town inhabited the vacant apartments the Jews left when they entered the ghetto. Two ghettos were established in Radom: the "large" ghetto, which was known as Wallowa, in the centre of town, and the "small" ghetto, also known as Glinice, in the suburbs, close to the industrial area. According to a German report, the Wallowa ghetto could contain 10,000,[7] yet 27,000 Jews were crammed into it. Five thousand Jews were crowded into the Glinice ghetto.

The Lodz and Warsaw ghettos were extremely crowded, not only because of the small space but also because the Germans expelled Jews from surrounding towns to those ghettos. In Radom, on the other hand, the German authorities did not transfer Jews from surrounding towns to the ghettos and did not allow Jews to go there. Yet, like the Adler family, many Jews, especially those who were from the Lodz area or who had relatives in town, arrived in the city and increased its population.

Unlike other ghettos, most Radom Jews worked outside their confined living quarters. Some worked directly for the official German authorities: the various departments of the civil administration, the several SS agencies (Amek and his brother worked in one of these), and the bases, supply depots and workshops of the military. Although most of the Jews worked as cleaners and handymen, some worked in their respective trades as mechanics, carpenters, electricians and tailors. Other Jews worked outside the ghettos in small private industries, such as a scrap company, a plant to process wood, and factories for making shoes, glue, cardboard, bricks and pots. The lack of space within the ghettos did not allow Germans to open workshops as they had in other places.

While Jews who worked for the German authorities and some who worked for private industries received a small salary, other workers in private industries received only food; still others received a meal and a small salary. Nevertheless, the big advantage of working outside the ghetto was the opportunity it gave Jews to trade with Poles on the black market. Exchanging goods and money for food prevented extensive hunger in the Radom ghettos. Other advantages included regularly getting news from outside and maintaining contact with other places.

Officially, Jews could work only for industries and workshops that contributed to the war effort or for other Jews within the boundaries of the ghettos. Within the ghettos the Judenrat, the Jewish council, was the largest employer. It employed more than five hundred people in various departments, which carried out German orders and managed Jewish life. The many bureaucratic positions were given to lawyers, engineers, teachers and students, who could not work in their profession. Their salary came from taxes and other levies imposed on the Jewish population.

The police and the health departments were the two largest. The main tasks of the 140 policemen included guarding the ghetto gates, accompanying the workers in private industries from the ghettos to their workplaces and back every day, and conducting night patrols. The health department operated an infirmary in the Glinice ghetto, and two hospitals and several infirmaries in the Wallowa ghetto. Both ghettos had sufficient nurses, physicians and dentists, but not enough medication or proper equipment. In mid-1942, the scarcity of medicine and equipment was so severe that when a typhus epidemic hit one of the hospitals, its entire medical staff became ill and some died.

The deadliest year during the Holocaust was 1942; more than three million Jews were killed.[8] High-ranking Nazi officials convened at the Wannsee conference in January 1942 to discuss the organization, coordination and implementation of the "Final Solution," the plan to murder all Jews. They assembled to make the ongoing process of eradicating the Jews centralized and more efficient. Six killing centres (Chełmno, Bełżec, Sobibór, Treblinka, Auschwitz-Birkenau and Majdanek) built on Polish soil operated that year. Bełżec, Sobibór and Treblinka were planned for the Jews who resided in the General Government. The mass murder of Polish Jews started in the spring. In July, Heinrich Himmler, head of the SS and the Gestapo, ordered that the removal of all Jews from the General Government be expedited. He allowed one exception: workers.

Even as they implemented their ideological views in the killing of all Jews, Nazi authorities took into consideration practical needs. The Germans had not subdued the Soviets as quickly as they expected. In 1942, they desperately needed to increase their armament production in order to continue fighting the war. However, they did not have a sufficient number of workers. German workers had been recruited to the east to help with the fighting, and the SS plan to use Soviet POWs could not be carried out as millions of them had perished in captivity.[9] As a result, Himmler allowed essential Jewish workers to remain alive temporarily. They were held in internment camps in five places, of which Radom was one.

Several weeks after that directive, in August 1942, the Germans liquidated the two Radom ghettos, sending most of their inhabitants to the gas chambers in Treblinka. The remaining Jews were interned in camps near their workplaces or in the Wallowa ghetto, which shrank to four streets. Amek's parents were in that small ghetto, which was officially named the "Jewish Forced Labour Camp Radom." Between six hundred and one thousand Jews lived there, labouring in facilities set in two buildings at the edge of the ghetto. They toiled in workshops for tailoring, shoemaking, carpentry and manufacturing of clocks, brushes, mattresses and gold. The workshops operated from 7:00 a.m. to 7:00 p.m., and the workers ate their lunch, which usually consisted of soup brought from the ghetto's kitchen, on site. Several hundred workers laboured for months to collect the property and material left behind by the deported Jews. Several dozen Jews worked for more than a year, sorting the clothing and linen of the deported Jews from the entire district, which were sent to Germany to welfare societies.

Most Jews who were not confined to the small ghetto lived in the Szkolna camp, which was built close to the local armament factory. Before the war, the Polish state owned the factory Wytwórnie Broni (Armament Development; unofficially known as Wytwórnia), which manufactured bicycles, Mauser guns and Vis pistols. Shortly after conquering Poland, the German authorities in Berlin debated wheth-

er to transfer the Polish armament industries to the Reich or to oper-
ate them in Poland for the benefit of the German army. They decided to keep them in Poland, giving them to private companies under
military supervision. The Austrian firm Steyr-Daimler-Puch became
the owner of the Radom armament factory, continuing the pre-war
armament production. Before the war the Poles had not employed
Jews in the factory, and in the beginning the Germans followed suit.
In the summer of 1941, when the war expanded to the east, the Germans admitted the first Jews to toil in maintenance works. The next
spring they started to exploit Jews in the production departments.
The civil administration was responsible for providing the number
of Jews required and giving them special work-cards so they could
leave the ghetto to work in the factory. In the summer of 1942, following the liquidation of the ghettos, the civil administration ceased
to be responsible for Jewish labour. Instead, the SS became its owner and rented out the labourers to the factory. Steyr-Daimler-Puch
paid 5 złotys for every male worker and 4 for every woman per day.
The company also had to rent guards to guard the Jewish slave labourers. Gradually the SS increased the number of Jews working in
the factory. Amek and his brothers were among them. By June 1943,
1,008 Jewish workers toiled in the factory, two-thirds of whom were
transferred from the city of Radom. Several hundred others were
transferred from liquidated ghettos and forced labour camps in the
district.[10]

After the liquidations of the ghettos, only "work Jews" could remain temporarily alive in the General Government. Nevertheless, being a "work Jew" did not guarantee survival. The geographical location and the type of work were crucial to one's chance of surviving.
Being a "work Jew" in Radom district increased the chances for survival. In the 1920s, the Polish government established several armament factories in an area called "the security triangle," located in the
centre of Poland, far from its borders, making it less vulnerable to
external attack. It remained an asset for the Nazis. Five of the eight

most important military factories in the General Government were in Radom district.[11] They became vital during the campaign for the increased armament production in 1942.

In the summer of 1943 the SS started to change its labour policy toward work Jews in the General Government. The uprisings in the ghettos of Warsaw (April–May 1943) and Białystok (August 1943), as well as in Treblinka (August 1943) and Sobibór (October 1943), made the SS leaders nervous about possible further unrest. In addition, personal rivalries within the Nazi hierarchy regarding the control of Jewish labour and the diminishing shortage of labour caused the destruction of Jews who worked in factories that manufactured equipment such as uniforms and shoes. Jews who worked in factories that produced weapons and ammunition were spared. In the summer and fall of 1943, most Jewish labour camps in the regions of Galicia, Lublin, Białystok, Warsaw and Krakow were eliminated, and most of their Jewish workers were killed. The largest known massacre at an individual location during World War II took place in Lublin district in November 1943. During two days known as the "Harvest Festival Massacre," more than 42,000 Jews were murdered.[12] In the Radom district, on the other hand, in November, "only" several hundred middle-aged women, old people, children and sick labourers were killed. As part of the new Jewish labour policy, the "Jewish Forced Labour Camp Radom" was liquidated. About 150 workers were shot and the others were transferred to the armament factories in the district. Most, like Amek's parents, were transferred to Szkolna, the camp of the local armament factory.

As part of SS reorganization, in January 1944 Szkolna became a concentration camp, administered by the SS in Majdanek, and the slave labourers officially became prisoners. Their hair was shaved and they received prisoners' suits and numbers. Their work in the factory remained the same, but discipline was harsher. SS guards replaced the factory guards. In July 1944, the Red Army conquered Lublin district and quickly advanced toward Radom. The military closed all the armament factories in the district, shipped their machines to the Reich and took the workers to Auschwitz or to the Reich. In the summer the Germans suffered defeats in France, the Soviet Union, Italy and Poland. They lost most of the areas they had conquered during the war. Yet they still hoped to create a weapon that could change the course of the war. In order to achieve this, they needed labour. Thus, even as they retreated they took their slave labourers with them. The Germans used trains when they had them and walked the slave labourers on foot when they did not.[13] The Jews from Radom, including Amek, experienced both forms of forced travel. Szkolna was closed on July 26, and its 3,000 inmates were marched 120 kilometres to Tomaszów Mazowiecki. After several days they boarded a train and were brought to Auschwitz-Birkenau.

Auschwitz-Birkenau had three major roles: as a killing centre, a source of human subjects for medical experiments and a reservoir of slave labourers. The subjects for experiments and the slave labourers were taken from transports and chosen through a selection made by Nazi physicians. Those not chosen were sent to their deaths in Birkenau's gas chambers.

The main criterion for slave labourers was that they be Jews between the ages of fifteen and forty-five in good physical shape. In 1942 and 1943, those selected to work were designated to toil primarily in Birkenau, where they had to build the gas chambers and crematoria, or in Buna, where they constructed the rubber manufacturing plants of IG Farben. From the summer of 1944, a large part of the labour force was not intended to remain at Birkenau but rather to be transported to Auschwitz subcamps or to camps in the Reich.

Until the transfer the arrivals registered as prisoners and their prisoner's number was tattooed on their forearm. The tattoo was unique to Auschwitz. In all concentration camps the prisoners received numbers, which were sewed to their striped uniform, but only in Auschwitz were those numbers also tattooed on their flesh. The order to tattoo was not given by the SS in Berlin but was a decision of the local commander. Apparently this practice started in late 1941 when the death toll was high and bodies could not be identified as their shirts were taken by other prisoners.

In Birkenau, Amek went through a selection on the ramp but was neither admitted to the camp nor tattooed. The case of Amek's transport, which arrived at Birkenau and left by train on the same day, was extremely atypical. Its uniqueness shows that during the Holocaust there were always unusual experiences. Those extraordinary cases were especially prevalent during the chaotic last year of the war when the Nazis acted in panic to avert their defeat, and the hierarchical structure within the SS was disintegrating.[14]

In that year Hitler reversed his 1941 policy to keep the territory of the Reich *judenrein*, free of Jews. In November 1941, the Germans had started to systematically expel the local Jews and did not bring Jewish slave labourers to the concentration camps in the Reich. Following continuous Allied air raids on factories producing aircrafts in the winter of 1944, German authorities decided to build underground factories to protect production. A large number of workers was needed.[15] Hitler allowed the relocation of 200,000 Jewish slave labourers to the Reich, and many new labour camps were built. They were attached administratively to a major concentration camp, but communications were bad and orders were not fulfilled. The daily number of prisoners doubled, and prisoners were transported from camp to camp.[16] Amek's transfers to and within the Reich were part of these developments.

The final year of the war was the most fatal for concentration camp prisoners. Hard physical work, harsh living conditions and death marches took the lives of many prisoners; such was the fate of Amek's father and brother. In his memoir, Amek vividly describes the severe living conditions he experienced during this time. These intolerable conditions, shared by all concentration camp prisoners, became worse in the last year of the war because of the Nazi haste to build more concentration camps and the lack of proper communications. Prisoners arrived at overcrowded camps where not all barracks were ready and straw and blankets did not suffice for all. Sanitary facilities were inappropriate and insufficient, increasing the incidence of stinging bugs and typhus epidemics. A constant shortage of food caused hunger, and shortages of winter clothes and shoes contributed to the high percentage of sick people, confounded by the lack of medical facilities.[17]

Amek was able to survive and rebuild a new life, first in Sweden and then in Canada. He raised a family and established a successful business. Like many survivors, Amek kept his memories to himself and began to talk only after the release of the movie *Schindler's List* (1993). The movie focused on survival through labour and contributed to the change in the public discourse to honour survivors. Amek gave his testimony to the Spielberg archive, created after the movie. Now he has written a memoir, which will make the story of his Holocaust ordeal and survival available for generations to come.

Idit Gil
The Open University of Israel
2017

ENDNOTES

1 Christopher R. Browning, *Nazi Policy, Jewish Workers, German Killers* (Cambridge: Cambridge University Press, 2000), 69–88.

2 Michal Unger, *Lodz: The Last Ghetto in Poland* (Jerusalem: Yad Vashem, 2005), 48–49.

3 Ibid., 64–65, 76.

4 "Identifying Marks for Jews in the Government General, November 23, 1939," in *Documents on the Holocaust: Selected Sources on the Destruction of the Jews of Germany and Austria, Poland, and the Soviet Union*, ed. Yitzhak Arad, Yisrael Gutman and Abraham Margaliot (Lincoln, NE: U of Nebraska Press, 1999), 178.

5 Dan Michman, *The Emergence of Jewish Ghettos during the Holocaust* (Cambridge: Cambridge University Press, 2011), 6–7, 70–87.

6 Zimerman Ing., "Radom: A Center of Industry," in *Radom Book*, ed. Avraham Shmuel Shtein (Tel Aviv: Irgun Yotzei Radom, 1962), 179–180 [Hebrew].

7 Yad Vashem Archive, O.53.101.65, Report on conditions in the city of Radom during the month of February 1941.

8 Christian Gerlach, *The Extermination of the European Jews* (Cambridge: Cambridge University Press, 2016), 99.

9 Adam Tooze, *The Wages of Destruction: The Making and Breaking of the Nazi Economy* (New York: Penguin, 2006), 155–157.

10 Idit Gil, "Intrigues and Conflicts of Interest as to the Exploitation of Jewish Labor in Radom, 1942–1943," in *Lessons and Legacies XII: New Directions in Holocaust Research and Education*, ed. Wendy Lower and Lauren F. Rossi (Evanston: Northwestern University Press, 2017), 396–397.

11 International Tracing Service Digital Collection, Militàrbefehlshaber im Generalgouvernement, 1.2.7.3, USHMM, 82181429, Military report #13 on the armament industry in the General Government, September 24, 1941.

12 Browning, *Nazi Policy*, 85–86.

13 Daniel Blatman, *The Death Marches: The Final Phase of Nazi Genocide* (Cambridge, Mass.: Belknap Press of Harvard University Press, 2011), 53.

14 Ibid., 55.

15 Michael Thad Allen, *The Business of Genocide: The SS, Slave Labour, and the Concentration Camps* (Chapel Hill, NC: University of North Carolina Press, 2002), 232–234.

16 Nikolaus Wachsmann, "The Dynamics of Destruction: The Development of the Concentration Camps, 1933–1945," in Jane Caplan and Nikolaus Wachsmann (eds.), *Concentration Camps in Nazi Germany: The New Histories* (New York: Routledge, 2010), 32–35.

17 Idit Gil, "Jewish Slave Laborers from Radom in the Last Year of the War: Social Aspects of Exploitation," in *Freilegungen: Spiegelungen der NS-Verfolgung und ihrer Konsequenzen* (Uncovered: A Sampling of Early Research Results from ITS Archival Holdings Mirroring NS-Persecution and its Consequences), eds. Rebecca Boehling, Susanne Urban, Elizabeth Anthony and Suzanne Brown-Fleming (Goettingen: Wallstein, 2015), 101–115.

To my father, my brother Josef, my grandparents, and my uncles, aunts and cousins who were murdered by the Nazis between 1939 and 1945. A special dedication to my brother Ben, who saved my life twice during our fight to survive in those terrible times.

To my oldest brother, Arthur, whom I was blessed to have with me for many years after the Holocaust. Sadly, Arthur, the last link to my past from my childhood, died on October 22, 2008, nine days after turning ninety. He passed on to a better world. May he rest in peace. I miss him.

To my mother, my friend — thank you for the love and courage you gave me before and after the war.

To my wife, Ruth, my children, Rose and Barry, their spouses, Jeff and Melissa, and my grandchildren, Evan, Staci, Jordan and Megan — thank you for being you.

And to my friends and family who encouraged me to write my story, I thank you from the bottom of my heart.

I will never forget any of you.

Author's Preface

During the war, I promised myself that if I survived and had a family of my own, I would not tell them about my experiences. I wanted to save them from knowing the horror and suffering that I had endured. I felt that my pain was a burden to carry on my shoulders, and it has left a lifelong scar. In any event, after the war, people avoided listening to us survivors. We were often called the derogatory term "Greenies," and I felt like we did not belong in the community. I felt humiliated, angry and ashamed to tell anyone I was born in Poland. If someone asked me where I came from, my answer was Sweden, which was not a lie, since I had come to Canada from Stockholm as a Swedish citizen and paid all the expenses as an immigrant. I realize now it was wrong to withhold the story of my suffering — the world must know and understand our history. I can't change the past, but I can help change the future.

In 1997, I was interviewed by Steven Spielberg's Survivors of the Shoah Visual History Foundation, which confirmed for me that every survivor must tell his or her story; the world must never allow the horror to happen again and must never be allowed to forget. Nine years later, in April 2006, I went on my first trip with the March of the Living, where I told my life story to educate youth about the Holocaust. This trip to Poland and Israel revived my feelings about the need for a homeland, and I will never forget what Rabbi Glenn Black and the march did for me — they released me from the heavy burden I had carried for sixty years.

This life story is not fiction. All the events that my family and I went through are true and documented. It is unimaginable that a civilized country like Germany, a leader in education and social life in Europe before the war, could allow the rise of the Nazi regime. It is unimaginable that the Nazis could murder millions of men, women and children in such a barbaric way. It is hard to believe that this would be anyone's destiny.

After the war, many Germans claimed, "We did not know," or "I was not a Nazi." But the photographs and records do not lie — they plainly show that a large portion of the population was satisfied with Adolf Hitler's achievements. Hitler promised them a Thousand-Year Reich. Saying "I did not know" is insulting to our intelligence, especially those of the survivors and the many nations that suffered. The deniers of the Holocaust are dangerous. They are liars. We still have thousands of eyewitnesses to prove the Holocaust happened, and I am one of them.

While we cannot bring back those who suffered and perished in Poland and other European countries, we nevertheless must honour their memory forever.

Four Brothers

My father, Simon Adler, lived in Radom, Poland, and in 1916 he went to Lublin on a business trip, where he met my mother, Fay. Mother was a pretty blond with long pigtails, blue eyes and a cheerful disposition. He fell in love at first sight. He was twenty-two years old and my mother was only sixteen and still in school, but he was determined that she would be his wife. With the blessing of her parents, my father waited until my mother turned seventeen and had finished high school.

They got married in February 1918 and settled in Lublin. Arthur, my oldest brother, was born the following October; my brother Ben was born two years later and Josef was born the next year. I was born at No. 2 Lubartowska Street in Lublin on April 20, 1928, the year before the Great Depression began. Many years later, my mother told me that she was unhappy being pregnant with me while having three other sons, one of them ten years older than I was. She confided that she had wanted to end the pregnancy but my father and grandfather were against it. When I was born, my maternal grandfather, Noah, was thrilled. Many of his friends asked him why, as he already had three grandchildren. He replied, "There is something special about this baby boy; he will be lucky for us." My one regret is that I share my birthday, April 20, with Adolf Hitler.

My father's parents, I later learned, had not attended their wedding, and they didn't come to my brothers' bar mitzvahs. I found out the reason after the war — my father was the third child, with an older brother and sister, and he had married out of turn, just as his father had before him. History had repeated itself. When my grandfather married out of turn, his parents were disheartened and disinherited him as punishment. The Adler family belonged to the Jewish aristocracy in Radom — they had a big tannery and leather factory and employed a lot of people. My father, too, was punished for disobeying his parents' wishes and marrying for love.

I saw my paternal grandfather, Max, maybe only six times. Once, when my father went on a business trip to Radom, he took me along with him and we stayed with my grandfather, who was six feet tall, had a waxed English moustache — narrow and upturned — and a short, well-trimmed beard. He never spoke to me or put his hand on my head. He was cold and reserved, and always elegantly dressed.

In 1933, we moved to the main street, at 53 Krakowskie Przedmieście, just around the corner from a park, where in winter we skated and sledded and in summer played ball. We had a good life, and my parents were very much in love. My father worked in the textile trade and was able to provide for his wife, four boys and in-laws. We lived in a nice part of the city in a comfortable apartment and we had a phone — the only one in the building. My mother was a lady of leisure. My parents enjoyed a busy social and cultural life, rich with Jewish theatres and movies, friends and relatives. We always had a live-in maid and my grandma directed the household. We rented a cottage in the countryside during July and August, in Nowy Dwór. My dad and granddad came out on Fridays and stayed until Monday morning. My parents had many friends there, and we had a *minyan*, a prayer quorum, on Shabbat. I always looked forward to the weekends.

Before the war, there was antisemitism but it affected us minimally. We did not feel discrimination as much as Jews did in the smaller towns and villages. Thirty per cent of the population of Lublin was

Jewish — close to 40,000 people — and we were well respected. Lublin was the centre of Judaism: the city was often called the Oxford of Jewish learning and the rabbis who graduated from the yeshiva were respected all over the world. I visited the yeshiva several times with my maternal grandfather, Noah. The building had over 120 rooms and one measured twenty by twenty feet. It was dedicated to Jerusalem and a model of the ancient temple — built to perfection — sat on a large table. I can still visualize its windows. My grandfather established a small synagogue and conducted the services on Rosh Hashanah and Yom Kippur. We had permanent seats assigned. We were Orthodox; how I missed that life, later. We looked forward to going to shul Friday nights and Saturday mornings, to the family lunches of gefilte fish and cholent and to being together on the holidays. There is no replacement for those times.

As a little boy, I used to go with my grandmother to the market to purchase chickens and fish for Shabbat. Before Passover, my grandmother and I would go to the bakery to supervise the baking of matzah for our home. Grandma Frieda was a religious woman, and I loved to listen to her stories. One in particular stands out. I asked, "What does God do all day?" Grandma answered, "He makes stepladders." "Why?" I asked. She answered, "Because as one side goes up, another side goes down in health and in wealth." This answer impressed me. Today, I realize how true it is: some people make fortunes and some lose them. People get sick and some get healthy. Life goes on.

In 1936, my grandfather Noah passed away at age seventy-seven. The night before his passing, he tutored my brother Ben in English. He spoke Polish, Russian and German as well. He had been a banker and a philanthropist; he was also a natural healer and many doctors sent patients to him. Grandpa Noah was fun to be with, and we boys had adored him. It felt as though the whole city mourned his death.

After Grandfather Noah's death, we moved to the city of Lodz, where my father did most of his business in the textile trade. He had wanted to move sooner but he respected my grandparents and did not want to uproot them from their life in Lublin, so he had been commuting by train.

Lodz was an industrialized city with a population of about 660,000, of whom over 230,000 were Jews. We lived at No. 68 Zachodnia Street, just around the corner from the Altshtot, or Old Town, synagogue, which was built in the 1860s. We kids went to a private school. As my father was in the textile industry, we were all elegantly dressed. Before the war, the middle and upper classes did not purchase ready-made men's and ladies' clothes. All clothes were custom-made, so the textile industry was very important and exported all over Europe. Twice a year, for Passover and Rosh Hashanah, I remember the ritual of my whole family ordering new, custom-made clothes, from shoes to hats.

My brothers were attentive to me. My brother Ben was seven years older than me, and Josef, four years older, so we had the most tension. I competed with Josef and we were both stubborn, but we still loved each other. Josef was extremely smart, an excellent student, and my parents had high hopes for him. Ben liked to keep to himself, always taking things apart and putting them together. He was musically inclined and played several instruments by ear. At nineteen years old, he was the youngest in his class to graduate from college as a textile engineer. Arthur joined my father in the business. He was always dressed to kill and loved having a good time. He was very popular with the young ladies and often brought them home to meet the family. I was not the academic type — sports and friends were on my mind more than studying.

I had a happy childhood and a loving family. While I feel I was robbed of my youth, I do cherish my memories of that time.

The Panic to Escape

In 1939, when we returned home from the summer holidays, the pending war was on everyone's mind. Only now can I imagine the feelings and worries the adults had at the time — some people still had scars from World War I. To us kids, at age eleven or younger, war was exciting, a novelty after seeing the battle pictures from World War I. In the countryside of Lublin, where we spent two months of our summers, ditches dug by soldiers some twenty-five years earlier were still visible. The adults felt differently about the war. Poland had been occupied by the German, Austrian and Russian armies, and Polish citizens had gone through hell.

Germany attacked Poland on September 1, 1939, at 4:45 a.m. Their army drove into Poland motorized and fully equipped for war. The Polish army was on horseback with hand-held lances, facing German tanks. Poland used World War I rifles and had a handful of old planes, most of which did not work, for battle against modern airplanes. The Polish army confiscated people's horses, automobiles, motorcycles and bicycles for the defence of the country. The Polish government stated that our country would defend each city to the last centimetre. But Warsaw surrendered just twenty-six days after the German invasion and the last Polish troops gave up nine days after that. Our soldiers were taken prisoner and sent to Germany for hard labour amid poor living conditions. While Poland was productive in agriculture and other industries, it did not have the foresight to defend its citizens. In the 1930s, the Polish government, instead of arming itself like any other European country, had been busy with its Jewish kosher "problems," debating, Should we allow the Jews to slaughter animals their way or our way?

It was amazing that a country the size of Poland, with a population of 33 million, including the largest Jewish population in Europe — 10 per cent — collapsed in a matter of weeks. Polish Jews started suffering from the first week of September 1939, which meant that our period of suffering during the war was longer than that of other European Jews. This was the beginning of the Polish Jewish massacre. Of Poland's 3.3 million Jews, 90 per cent would perish at the hands of the Nazis. Poland was chosen by the Nazis to create the biggest Jewish cemetery in the world.

The panic to escape from Lodz was unbelievable. As the Germans approached, my brother Ben had followed the crowds until he found himself in the capital, Warsaw. Ben looked up a cousin of my father's and spent a few weeks in the defence of Warsaw. The city fought tremendously with the little it had — no water, electricity or other supplies. When we were reunited with Ben, he described to us how women in elegant mink coats were cutting meat from dead horses on the streets and how he drank water from the Vistula River, which flowed through the city.

Only one week after the Nazis invaded Poland, their forces captured Lodz. It was on this day, September 8, 1939, that we began our hard life under the Nazi occupation. By mid-November, all Jews had to wear an armband, which was replaced about a month later with a yellow star inscribed with "Jude," worn on the left side of the chest and on the back for identification. A curfew was imposed: we had to be off the streets by 7:00 p.m. If we saw a Nazi approach on the sidewalk, we had to step down, bow and take our hats off. If not, we would be beaten on the spot. All Jewish schools had to be closed. Businesses were confiscated and given to the *Volksdeutsche*, ethnic

Germans. Jews were taken off the streets for manual labour, regardless of age or gender. My father was picked up one day to load coals. He came home late, dirty, hungry and exhausted. If a religious man with a beard and sidelocks was picked up, his hair was forcibly cut off, which was humiliating to an Orthodox Jew. Jewish women were taken off the street and made to clean soldiers' washrooms using their underwear. Food was rationed and life became intolerable.

We had seen lots of German-Jewish refugees of Polish descent arriving in 1938, so we thought we knew what to expect. But then we heard stories about Hitler and his band of criminals having no respect for human lives. Nobody could explain how anyone could do such things to another person, especially to children and the elderly. The rumours were alarming. It was hard to believe or explain the behaviour of the Nazis.

One morning in November 1939, the SS poured asphalt and gasoline into the beautiful synagogue to which we belonged, the Altshtot, and set it on fire. Black smoke poured through the windows. I will never forget standing across the street and watching the burning synagogue with tears in my eyes.

Our lives had changed overnight. As a young boy, I was angry and it was hard for me to understand the situation we were in. We became prisoners in our apartments, with no knowledge of what would happen in the future. I missed getting together with my friends and family on the weekends, Shabbat and holidays. I missed school even though I was not academically inclined. I missed going to synagogue on Shabbat with my father and brothers, going to movies and having a social life.

Another order was issued: if anyone had American dollars or British sterling currency, they had to turn it in. If the Nazis found any in your home, you could be shot. My parents had to think about what to do with their foreign currency, which was hidden, along with their valuables, in a sliding secret compartment inside their modern bedroom set. One day the Nazis came to our building and with loudspeakers announced they had come to pick up the foreign currency. My father put all our US dollars and British sterling currency in the oven to burn. Luckily, our neighbour was present, took the money and hid it all. We needed that money to support us.

It did not take long for some of the Polish women to pick up friends in the German army. Our young Polish maid brought her new boyfriend, a German Wehrmacht sergeant, to the apartment. The situation was uncomfortable and it felt shocking to be in the apartment with a German in uniform but we didn't dare say anything, even in our own home. She brought her German boyfriend to our home more and more often.

My father was looking for a way to get out of Lodz. Food was rationed and Jewish businesses confiscated. How could we adjust to this way of life? Rumours spread fast that a Jewish ghetto was being created in Lodz and Jews were going to be brought in from all the small surrounding towns.

In February 1940, the ghetto was created and we had to move to a smaller apartment in a different part of the city. We left everything we had to the maid. Now, as an adult, I can relate to my parents' feelings — leaving all their possessions to a stranger, one who had a German boyfriend, a Wehrmacht soldier, no less. But, she had been with us for several years. We had brought her from Lublin and now she became the owner of all our possessions. We took only what we could carry and left behind a twenty-year-old household established by my parents.

My eldest brother, Arthur, who was twenty-one, was in danger of being taken to Germany for hard labour. So he and two other young men, with the blessings of their parents, escaped from Lodz. Arthur's objective was to get to Romania and from there to England, as my mother had a sister living in London. My aunt had a large family and I had many older cousins. I was so upset that Arthur did not say goodbye to me, as we were very close. My parents calmed me down with the explanation that Arthur had had to leave at night for his safety. I missed him terribly all through the war, wondering what had happened to him.

When Ben got back to us in Lodz, my parents and a few friends decided to leave the city. It took a lot of planning and lots of money to bribe the right people to smuggle us out. My father smartly insisted he pay at the end of the trip, for safety reasons. We travelled by night in a large trailer with the other two families hidden in the back behind some furniture. Each time we were stopped at a German checkpoint on the highway, we felt, this is it. A trip like this took a lot of nerve and was especially hard on my grandmother, who had a weak heart and was over eighty years old. Yet, miracles do happen, and I believe in them. The best proof? I am here, alive.

My Introduction to Misery

After a stressful night trip we arrived in Warsaw in the morning. The other two families who had travelled with us went their own way. We went to my father's cousin's home and luckily found an empty apartment next door. Apartments were scarce. We moved into Nowolipki 21, on the third floor of a big block of apartments surrounding a large courtyard.

Aside from the same 7:00 p.m. curfew as in Lodz, life in Warsaw was different. Here, we had to register for coupons to purchase food. There were long lines everywhere. Yet, my family did not suffer as much as others because we could afford to purchase some food on the black market. My mother, with her pure blond hair and blue eyes, could pass as a gentile and could leave the Jewish area. About twice a week, she would go to the black market to get some food.

The area we lived in comprised wall-to-wall people rounded up from the small cities and villages surrounding Warsaw and imprisoned in a yet-to-be formed ghetto — the wall was being built. The Nazi plan, I learned later, was to have all the Jewish people from around Warsaw in one place for future transportations.

Since the Nazis had come in, schooling was illegal. Where we lived, I was appointed to entertain a class of seven-year-olds in the illegal day school within our block of apartments. This type of job marked the beginning of my leadership roles in organizations I would be involved with throughout my life.

One day, I was walking with a friend of mine outside our building when a German teenager dressed in black shorts with a brown shirt and a swastika on his left arm — a member of the Hitler Youth — walked by and hit my friend without any provocation. Well, I could not take it. My blood just boiled. It took a second to respond, but I jumped the teenager and hit him so hard he lost his balance and fell on the pavement. I was tall and strong for my age. I banged his head against the asphalt until blood came from his mouth. Bystanders tore me away. I had to hide for several weeks because the Germans were looking for me.

Another time, I refused to take my hat off for a German soldier, so he threw me against the wall of a building and beat me. My legs just buckled. When I came to, all I could see was a pair of large legs in front of me. From that day on, I never wore a hat, not even after the war, during the cold winters in Sweden and Canada.

Life in Warsaw became more difficult. The Germans opened the Warsaw ghetto in October 1940. More people were brought in from the countryside and surrounding small towns and villages. Children begged for food. The streets were soon littered with dead bodies, even as the pickup wagon constantly collected the dead for burial. Warsaw was my first encounter with ghetto life, an introduction to misery and persecution. It is impossible to fully describe the entirety of the injustice done to our people. Even today, I have the whole picture in front of me and it is hard to believe what I know to be true. It is all behind me now, some seventy years later, but those images have remained with me for life. I still have nightmares.

Life was so unbearable that my father talked about leaving Warsaw. Soon, rumours raced through the ghetto that the gates would be closing for good. Once they were closed, it would be very difficult to leave, so my father made the decision to depart immediately. Fortunately, we had the financial means to make such a move. My father decided it would be to Radom, his birthplace. His father, two sisters and two brothers still lived there. It took money and effort to leave by train with false permits and identity documents. If caught, we would have been punished with death. The Warsaw ghetto was closed to the outside world on November 15, 1940. We had left two weeks before, just in time.

We took the night train, a trip of several hours; it was easier to travel by night because the military traffic was lighter and our chances of not being stopped were better. My parents, my grandmother, Ben, Josef and I sat in the train's third-class carriage because the second- and first-class carriages were reserved for the German military. At every stop, we had to show our forged travel permits. My grandmother was uncomfortable and scared. The stress and fear we all felt was palpable.

We eventually arrived at my grandfather's apartment in Radom. It was a little tight, but Radom, like any other large city, was full of refugees from surrounding small towns and communities trying to find space and safety from persecution. My grandfather strongly believed that when Britain entered the war, the fighting would be over within a few months. He was a conservative and acted like an Englishman.

For the next five months, we experienced some tranquility; we had more freedom and peace. Radom had a large Jewish population before the war and it had become larger due to the influx of Jews from surrounding areas. It was not paradise or like life before the war, but we managed to sustain some quality of family life.

My brother Ben befriended a younger man whose father was a watch repairman. Being so mechanically inclined, Ben was fascinated with the mechanism of watches and picked up the profession in no time. He also befriended a young lady, Etta, and soon insisted on marrying her.

Then, by April 1941, the ghetto in Radom was established. At first, it was easier to endure than the ghetto in Lodz or Warsaw, but with the influx of Jews from other communities, it soon also became crowded. With a shortage of apartments and work, the picture started to look like Warsaw again — people begging and sleeping in the streets, with some never waking up.

In the ghetto, the Nazis formed a Jewish police force. Ben was invited to join but declined. We were allowed to go out only if we had work outside the ghetto. We had to have official papers showing our place of work, were forced to wear white armbands with a blue Star of David and had a 7:00 p.m. curfew. After that time, we kids congregated on the stairway of our apartment building to entertain ourselves.

Through the Jewish Council, who were in charge of the ghetto's administration (under Nazi orders), Ben got a job as a superintendent and handyman in the German Security Service, or "SD," which occupied an entire six-storey building. The Germans took a liking to him; sometimes he came home with bread, salami or cheese. He also received a bicycle and special papers permitting him to leave the ghetto at any time. The bike had a plate on it saying: "This bicycle belongs to the Department of Special Forces," and nobody could claim it. It was unusual for a Jew to possess a bicycle, but its purpose was to allow Ben to go to work on the spur of the moment.

Ben had a gift. People always took a liking to him. He was handy and inventive, and had built an AM and shortwave radio at age fourteen. He was a mechanical genius and could fix anything. He mastered watchmaking and photography, and he even fixed guns. I asked Ben if he could get me a job as his assistant. He asked his boss and sure enough, I became Ben's helper. He showed me how to install electrical lines and outlets, make window blinds and fix small appliances. We worked together on many projects.

Working in a military building, we saw Poles who had been brought in from the underground organizations and from the Polish intelligentsia — leaders, lawyers, priests, doctors and teachers. They were interrogated and tortured; we saw them beaten beyond human imagination. Their screams still ring in my ears.

In April, before I turned thirteen, my father arranged for an elderly man to come twice a week to teach me for my bar mitzvah. I was not a great student and I was rebellious. Finally, the Shabbat closest to April 20 arrived and my father, grandfather and my two brothers

took me to a *shtiebl*, a small, private house of worship, for the services, which had to be held in secret. There was a *minyan* to serve as
my witnesses. The service was quick and short: I was called to the Torah, I said the prayers, a bottle of wine was opened and it was over. At
home, we had lunch, just the family, and I became a man in the eyes
of God, my family and fellow Jews. At the same time, I also became a
political prisoner of, and threat to, the Third Reich.

~

The days and months passed and we hoped for a quick end to the war
and our miseries so we could return to our normal lives. One day in
August 1942, we were awoken at 5:00 a.m. by yelling and screaming
and banging on doors; it put the fear of death into us. The first thing
my father did was to gather all his foreign money and throw it out the
window into the backyard. The ghetto in Radom was surrounded by
SS soldiers, who started to round us up. We were ordered out of the
apartment and we had to leave all our possessions and assemble on
the street. The selection began instantly. Some went to the left and
some to the right. I shook from fear.

I was selected to join a group with my grandfather, grandmother,
two uncles, three aunts, my parents, my sister-in-law, and my two
brothers, as well as Etta's mother and her three siblings. The officer in
charge, for whom Ben and I worked, spotted Ben and ordered him to
step out from the line and to follow him. Ben replied that he wouldn't
go without his parents, wife and brothers. For us, because of Ben, the
order was changed and we all left the line immediately. That day, Ben
saved us from going to the Treblinka death camp.

Tragically, my grandparents, uncles and aunts could not be saved.
I cannot describe the feelings and looks as the SS officer separated us
from the rest of the family. Every time I think of this scene, I get shiv-
ers down my spine, perhaps the result of guilt for leaving my grandparents and the rest of our relatives behind.

The ghetto was reduced to about 2,000 people. All the others were marched away to the train station for transport to, at that time, the unknown. Those who remained, like my parents, were left in the smaller ghetto. I was taken, along with Josef and Ben and Ben's wife, Etta, outside the city to brand new barracks at Szkolna Street. This new labour camp had been established at an old government factory called Wytwórnia to provide guns, artillery and bicycles for the German army. The camp consisted of separate barracks for men and women, one barrack for showers for men and one for women, a kitchen and separate outhouses.

We worked in twelve-hour shifts from 7:00 a.m. to 7:00 p.m. every day. Our meals consisted of black coffee in the morning, a bowl of soup for lunch and a slice of black bread and coffee in the evening. Twelve hours of work is a long day on rations like that. On Sundays we received a treat — a goulash and some meagre meat with potatoes. We had showers once a week and we felt like zombies, day in and day out.

Each of the departments had a German manager and the one we had was not too bad, but two or three times a week, he would select a young Jewish woman and bring her to his office for his personal pleasure. This became widely known. The hardest place to work was in the casting department for heavy artillery. With the heat from the ovens, conditions were unbearable. I was lucky to be assigned to a power machine producing parts for bicycles. I was so fascinated with all the machinery that in a short time, I was appointed as assistant to the floor foreman and helped him fix the breakdowns. The floor fore-man was Polish and had a hunchback. He was not a bad man and, because he liked me, he taught me on all the machines. This gave me hope that I would be able to get through the war as a mechanic.

As for life in the barracks, it was hot in the summer and cold in the winter. There was no ventilation; the windows were permanently shut. The wooden double bunks had mattresses consisting of burlap stuffed with straw. One electric bulb hung from the ceiling, offering no more than forty watts. The barracks housed eighty to one hundred people.

Arriving back at the barracks after work, following lights-out, we talked and reminisced quietly about our past lives and the future we might have. We sang songs. We cried, we laughed. We had to do our best to keep our spirits and morale high. I was introduced to many Yiddish songs and jokes for the first time — at home, my grandmother was the only one who spoke Yiddish, and I had always responded to her in Polish. We still believed it wouldn't be long until our liberation. My biggest assets were having my two brothers with me and knowing my parents were nearby.

Occasionally, we received parcels from my parents, who were in the small ghetto. Because it was less closely guarded, my mother was able to sneak out to trade some bread for whatever she had left, and she sent it to us. There were couriers between our new camp and the small ghetto who smuggled the goods inside.

Ben became the official watch repairman for the outside guards. He did the repairs on Sundays and they paid him with bread or cigarettes. There were no replacement parts — he made many by hand. The Ukrainian guards were brutal and hated the Jews, but they were crazy about watches. Each wore three to six watches on their arms. The guards did not look very civilized to us. Most were farm boys with hate on their minds.

In the spring of 1943, the Nazis brought a group of about one hundred Jews from the city of Lublin to our camp. The Lublin ghetto had been liquidated in the spring of 1942; most of its inhabitants were sent to the Bełżec death camp, but some were transferred to a forced labour camp in a Lublin suburb and eventually ended up in Radom. I knew one family quite well, as their youngest daughter, Zosia, who was my age, had been my classmate and my first puppy love. We found out from them what had happened to the Jews of Lublin who had not been killed in Bełżec — more than a year later, nearly all of the rest had been sent to the Majdanek concentration camp and were murdered. The group brought to Radom had been rewarded for working for the Germans as tailors and shoemakers. Their arrival and the Lublin ghetto's liquidation weighed heavily on all of us and we feared the future, but our elders assured us that as long as we were working, the Nazis needed us — so we were safe.

We experienced some happiness in November, when the small ghetto in Radom was liquidated and all the residents were brought to our camp. We were glad to be reunited with our parents. My mother and sister-in-law were in the women's barracks and we could communicate with them only during the day, at work, since we all worked in the bicycle department.

In January 1944, the Radom labour camp was re-classified as a subcamp of Majdanek and transformed into a concentration camp — double barbed wire surrounded us, as did towers with guards armed with machine guns. Other guards — Ukrainian men in black SS uniforms, some of whom could not even speak German despite serving the Nazis — patrolled the area with dogs. Now we were assembled twice a day, rain or shine, for the long *Appell*, the head count. At times, we stood for two hours while the Germans checked the count. The trip from the barracks to the factory was a few kilometres. Since we needed time for the walk so we could start on time for the twelve-hour shift, the days became a sixteen-hour ordeal. It was especially hard in the winter.

One day at roll call, it was discovered that a young man had escaped from the camp. The following Sunday we were all assembled in the courtyard and the family of the escaped man was put in the middle of a circle. An officer who was in charge of the guards, dressed in a black uniform and an eye patch, instructed the family, consisting of husband and wife and a teenaged boy and girl, to kneel. He went behind them and warned us, "This will happen to you and your family if you try to escape!" Then he drew his pistol and fired shots into the back of each head before him. The victims' last words were, "Shema Yisrael" (Hear O Israel), part of a central prayer in Judaism. Those words will stick with me for the rest of my life. Since the war, every time I attend a synagogue and hear the *Shema* prayer, I see the horror all over again. It is a heavy burden. This was the first time I had seen people executed. Corpses in the ghetto did not bother me as much as this execution did.

Months later, in early 1944, two young men, brothers I knew from the ghetto, one my age and the other four years older, disappeared from the camp without a trace. A few months later, on a dirt road just outside the camp, a truck was making a delivery when the rear wheels on one side sank into a hole. Well, this started a whole commotion: dogs were brought in, the hole was made wider and soldiers with guns lowered themselves inside and discovered a bunker and a tunnel. There, they found the Zuckerman siblings and three others. The tunnel had been progressing well and the group was already outside the camp, but they had lost their sense of direction and had begun digging upwards instead of continuing straight. The whole camp was assembled. The Commandant, a middle-aged officer from the SS, made a speech. "I am in a good mood today," he said, "and this is a lucky day for the boys." He ordered the tunnel to be filled in and gave the boys fifty lashes each. Their skin ran with blood. We all had to watch.

Through all the hardships I felt blessed being together with my father and two brothers; it made me feel a little more secure. It is hard to know what my father was feeling as he looked at his three sons and worried for their future. Now, as a parent and grandparent, I can imagine what my father felt at the time.

On many occasions, as I watched my family's deteriorating health and fading will to live, I, too, felt like giving up and ending the suffering. But we Adlers are of strong will and beliefs. My motto was, if the Nazis did not put a bullet in me, I would survive. I hoped my family felt the same way.

Hanging On

We had hoped we were safe in Radom, working for the Germans in the factory, but one bright morning near the end of July 1944, orders came for the camp to be closed. We had one hour to get ready and could take only what we could carry. We did not know where we were going.

The journey took four days; we walked most of the time through villages and small towns. We weren't given any water or food. We collected water from ditches and ate what we could find during the night's rest. All around us, people hit the ground from exhaustion and hunger. Shots were fired at those who fell. We rested at night, not for our sake but for the sake of the guards. Most of them were unfit for the front line due to illness or age. It did not take much for them to shoot a Jew if he stepped out of line, even accidentally. We heard the rifle shots constantly and the group shrank. By the second day, the number of prisoners had decreased. I think we lost more than two hundred people on this march.

The Polish population stood by and watched us marching through their towns. Some shook their heads, some smiled and some showed a closed fist. This part of my life I will never forget. It took about four misery-filled days to reach our destination: Auschwitz. Yet, fate was good to me because I can't claim to have been an inmate of Auschwitz-Birkenau.

We were ordered out onto a concrete platform next to the rail tracks and were greeted by SS officers and soldiers with guns and dogs. The selection started immediately: older women and children to one side, and able women for work to the other. My mother and Etta were selected for the group of working women. It was hard enough for me to say goodbye to my mother; I felt angry watching my father, who had never been separated from his wife, forced from her side. It was the most unforgiving scene I had ever endured. Men were also separated — men who looked older and in bad shape were made to join the group of older women and children.

When the officer approached us, we tried to look fit. I was asked my age. I answered, "Seventeen." Being tall, and only a year younger than that, I passed for seventeen easily, especially alongside my father and two brothers. Women were screaming about their children being torn away. Some families did not want to be separated, so soldiers used canes to hit people for not obeying their commands. German shepherds barked loudly and bared their teeth. The women, children and older men were taken away immediately, assembled in fives. They were made to march to Birkenau, three kilometres away. It is hard to forget seeing others go through the selection, and it was an indescribable feeling to see friends, with whom we had gone through so much in the past few years, walk away to the unknown. The group of fit women was taken away next and we men remained on the platform for several hours into the evening.

While we waited, another transport arrived with Jews and we watched as they were treated like cattle sent to be slaughtered. We saw a Nazi officer make a selection. This one man had the power to decide between life and death over helpless men, women and children. Yet, he was just a regular human being — if this man had taken off his uniform, he would have blended into the crowd and looked no different from us prisoners.

At Auschwitz, we were not registered with tattooed numbers on our arms, as we were only in transit. Finally, we received a cup of watery soup and a slice of black bread, and eventually a train arrived.

We were loaded in, about one hundred men per car. I had watched my family being torn apart and degraded, and I had feared for my life. I was heartbroken, but I had been hardened, and I had learned not to cry.

On the train from Auschwitz, we tried to guess where we were going and what future to expect. We tried to be calm and hoped for the best. The trip took a day and a half. We were packed like cattle, and if you had to relieve yourself, it had to be on the spot. Words cannot describe the smell and conditions. We stopped in Prague, the capital of Czechoslovakia. Our small windows were covered with barbed wire but we could look out. When I did, I thought, "When this is all over, I will be able to tell my friends I was in Czechoslovakia." Then I cried that this was how I was travelling.

After several hours, the doors finally opened and we received a slice of bread and a cup of coffee. The doors were then closed again and we left the station. After two days of misery and not knowing our destination, we arrived in Stuttgart, Germany. The final destination was Vaihingen, a town about thirty kilometres away that was also the site of a brand new concentration camp — a subcamp of the Natzweiler concentration camp. There were only four barracks, five hundred men in each, and on the double bunk beds, the mattresses were filled with straw. The two windows were permanently shut. I saw a wooden, round heating stove with a pipe in it that led to the roof, and a bare light bulb hanging down. We later used the pipe from the stove to kill the bugs on our shirts by pressing that part of the shirt to the hot pipe — the sound of barbequing lice was amusing to us but we had to be careful not to burn the shirt. Outside was a wooden shack that functioned as a toilet and another for showering. There was also a kitchen.

The camp was surrounded by a double barbed-wire fence with a five-foot space between the fencing. There were four towers, each holding an SS man with a large machine gun. Between the wire fences, an SS man patrolled with a dog. Outside the camp, there was a gatehouse with guards to protect us, supposedly, from intruders.

I was assigned to the same barracks as my father and brothers. We were given a shower and sprayed with disinfectant powder, and then we received blue-and-white uniforms consisting of a pair of pants, a shirt, a round hat and a pair of wooden shoes. The clothing was made of wool. It was hot in the summer but not nearly warm enough for the winter, and felt rough on the skin.

We had been brought in to remove all the stray bricks after Allied bombardments, to clean the nearby city and to work in the factories. My family and I volunteered as mechanics and were assigned to a construction site located in an old salt mine to build an underground factory for airplanes. Our rations for the day consisted of a cup of coffee in the morning, a bowl of soup for lunch and a slice of bread and a cup of coffee in the evening. The shifts were twelve hours per day. One week was day work; the next, night work.

In the morning, we were woken at 5:00 a.m., two hours before work began, for the *Appell*. Roll call always took place before we went to work and after we returned to camp. Twelve hours of work plus the roll call before and after meant fourteen to sixteen hours per shift, depending on the mood of the Nazi commander.

Life worsened as time progressed, and we had a very hard time getting used to the terrible conditions. One week, shower privileges became scarcer (and colder) and changes of uniforms became few and far between. In the winter, we wore empty cement paper bags from the construction site underneath our clothing to keep us warm. You had to learn how to survive, but who could get used to the mental and physical torture, abuse and starvation? We were barely human anymore. People stole and did whatever they could to survive. Hunger can change people into animals, possessed with an uncontrollable urge to survive.

After a sixteen-hour day, still hungry after our so-called dinners, we tried to keep our sanity by reminiscing about the good old days at home with our families, the Shabbats, holidays and social events and dinners and dreams for the future. The Nazis could not control my thoughts and they could not deprive me of my dreams. I would think of this as I fell asleep. I had a beautiful past, and I dreamed of a life without pain and starvation. I hated to open my eyes in the morning. We were all getting weaker and some were getting sicker. Friends went to sleep and never woke up.

On Sundays my brother Ben fixed watches for the guards and officers, and that service helped us survive. I observed that the Germans often favoured certain Jewish workers among us. In my opinion, this was meant to ease their conscience.

By September 1944, we heard bombardments more often and much closer. After a while, my unit was assigned to a cleanup detail. We would go into Stuttgart after air attacks and clean the streets of the rubble of bricks, furniture and other debris. One day we walked to work and realized that the Nazi escort who usually accompanied us was not there. We went back and found him and his gun lying on the ground. It looked like he had suffered a heart attack. We picked him up and carried him back to camp. Later, I was criticized for not using the opportunity to escape. But where could we have gone in the middle of Germany, in our uniforms and shaved heads, looking like walking skeletons, with no money and no papers?

Frequently, on the way to the city, we found shot-down American aircraft, body parts, photographs, money, cigarettes, chocolates and other personal and military items. Cleaning up these disasters made us feel sorry for the pilots and crew. They had been trying to put an end to the atrocity and finish the war and instead suffered terrible deaths. We tended to their remains with tears rolling down our cheeks.

One day, my father got sick and had to stay behind for a few days. When the German overseer watching the crew asked me where my father was, I responded that he was sick and in camp. The next day, the overseer brought me two aspirins, an orange and a piece of bread, saying, "Take it home to your father." I will never forget him. This showed me that there were some Germans with consciences.

In late October 1944, just as it felt like we had gotten settled at the Vaihingen camp, we were shipped in cattle cars to a transit point called Kornwestheim, in southern Germany, a couple of hundred kilometres from Dachau. We were actually very sorry to leave Vaihingen, and the worst part of this trip was that I didn't know where we were going. There was no change of clothes and no showers. We arrived at a small subcamp of Natzweiler, where the barracks were crammed wall to wall. Beating and punishments were daily sport for the guards. We had to avoid all contact with the German personnel — a wrong look could cost us our lives or a severe beating. We had to become hard and determined and avoid confrontation by not bringing attention to ourselves. But at night, we showed our anger and cried out for help to God. While I felt that God was listening, He was taking his sweet time to listen in my case. I had never in my young life wished to kill anybody but I prayed for our guards to drop dead. I kept promising myself that with God's help, their time would come and we would be alive to talk about their deaths.

We moved mountains of large stones from one place to another without reason or logic. My mind wandered. Why was all this happening to us? Was there no one in heaven to punish the guilty? I came to the conclusion that I had to accept this as part of life and that there was nothing I could do but hang on until the last breath in my body. Maybe this horrible period would pass. I looked at my father and brothers and asked myself many times: Are those bodies my relatives? I am sure I looked the same to them. This, to date, was the worst chapter of our imprisonment. We feared for our lives. If I hadn't had my father and two brothers, I don't know what I would have done or what would have happened to me. What kept us alive were stories, especially jokes. In spite of feeling near death, we still told jokes, and we laughed and cried at the same time. Conversations like this were part of my salvation.

We spent about five hard, miserable months in this horrible place. Then, the Nazis separated us — Ben and me from my father and Josef

— and put us on different cattle trains to be transported to Dachau, not far from Munich. The trip seemed to take forever, though in reality, it ended up being six hours. As the iron wheels turned, to me they made a sound: "Hang on! Hang on! Hang on!"

It was a relief to be let out of the cramped rail car and breathe some fresh air when we arrived at Dachau. Dachau was a large camp with about 30,000 prisoners. It had one gas chamber, which was not in use, and two crematoria, which were. The counting began, and everyone received a red triangle with a number to put on the left side of their clothing, indicating they were a political prisoner. We were assigned to barracks, each of which held different nationalities. Built in 1933 to hold political opponents of the Nazi regime, Dachau was the first concentration camp, and others were modelled on it.

Ben and I picked a bunk to be together. We didn't know where Josef or our father was. The next morning, someone told us that my father's body had been taken off the train on the way there. He had died at fifty-one years old, in his prime — a tragic ending for a fine human and a wonderful father and husband. Whenever I think of him, tears come to my eyes. Josef, we heard, had tried to escape but was caught and shot. In all the years of imprisonment I could never shed a tear, but this time, I could not control myself. Ben told me not to cry, or we would be next. How much longer could we last? At that moment, I felt that Ben was my greatest asset. From that time on, we became closer, developing such a strong bond that we depended on each other's support to cling to life. We did not know the fate of my mother and sister-in-law. Now, with the terrible news about my father and brother, in my mind, only two of us remained from the whole family, although we hoped that our older brother, Arthur, was safe in England.

Our will to live was strong, however, and served as an ever-present reminder that we must go on. Every day, I saw men giving up the struggle to survive, just lying down to die. All this was hard to accept for a sixteen-year-old. My eldest brother was gone, and my father and my brother Josef were dead. Where was my mother? Was she alive in a camp somewhere? What had we done to deserve such a fate?

My generation had a hard time adjusting after liberation, and nobody helped us with any kind of therapy. After the war, someone told me that the human body and mind are stronger than steel. There is some truth to it. The punishment we went through can never fully be described.

Life in Dachau was not hard, but it was monotonous. Even though there was little to do all day, we were getting weaker; morale was deteriorating and some of us became sicker. Prisoners were dying daily. Perhaps this was the reason we were left alone. Ben got sick with typhus and he was admitted to the so-called hospital, which had one doctor but no medicine. Aspirin was the most popular pill when you went to see the doctor. For any ailment, you received an Aspirin.

When I sometimes go back in my thoughts to that miserable period of my life, I asked myself how I survived this nightmare. What went through my mind? I was hungry and exposed to the point that I heard hissing sounds, which drove me crazy. My mind was the only part of my anatomy still working, and I believed in my destiny and survival.

I missed Ben. I missed my dad and Josef. I hated to think of my mother, not knowing her situation. I hoped Arthur had made it safely to Romania and was in England by now. I was not permitted to visit Ben but I made sure to get information on his progress. I was happy he held his own and was relieved that he was still alive.

During the years of imprisonment in the camps, I learned to pray to God about our future. I prayed for the safety of us all. In Dachau, when Ben was taken to the hospital and I was alone, I prayed to God and hoped my mother, sister-in-law, Arthur, Ben and I would survive and be reunited. I made a promise for the future: I would not be greedy and would be honest and respect others. "Please let us survive, dear God, and let's all meet in Palestine." I had resolved never to return to Poland to live. Why Palestine? Before the war, I was told so many times, "Jew, go to Palestine!" There must be something to it, I thought, and that was the place to go find some peace, where the world would leave us Jews alone.

On April 26, 1945, the authorities at Dachau selected about 1,500 inmates and told us we would be exchanged for German prisoners. I refused to go. I wanted to stay close to Ben but it was not my decision. We boarded a first-class train and were given Red Cross parcels. This was the first time in six years of imprisonment that we had received Red Cross parcels. The Nazis had received these parcels, which were meant for us, but had kept them. The mood was light; we were headed to freedom. Except my mind was still in the camp with Ben.

When we arrived at the Austrian border, the train stopped and we all had to disembark. We heard artillery shots in the distance. The Nazis pushed us into a nearby valley and four machine guns surrounded us. Panic came over me. It crossed my mind that this must be the end. I spoke to two other boys my age, saying we must do something. "Let's try to escape; we have nothing to lose," I told them. Those machine guns were not there for display or decoration.

That day, there was no sun. It was grey and the grass was tall. We started to crawl out of the canyon. We got lucky and escaped. For two days, we passed through farms and villages, several of them deserted, searching for food. I saw banks with open safes and German money lying around for the taking. But our focus was food and finding the American army. On the second night, we had to rest, so we crept into a farmer's barn and fell asleep, exhausted. We were woken by the promising sound of heavy artillery so close and yet so far for us to reach. Soon, we believed, we would be free.

Reunions

The next morning we heard the sound of heavy tanks moving on the highway nearby. Looking out, we saw five-star insignia and soldiers who were not in German uniforms. We went out to the road and the whole column stopped and looked at us as if we were from another world. They had never seen sixteen-year-old boys resembling skeletons. One American soldier was of Polish background and we were able to communicate with him. We told him where we had come from, and they felt so sorry for us that they gave us Hershey chocolate bars and canned milk. The American soldiers meant well, but it was the wrong thing for us to eat. We were in very bad shape and hungry, but our stomachs could not digest the richness. I hate to describe the results and we did not have a change of clothes. I do not know the exact number of prisoners who died after liberation by being fed the wrong foods (not maliciously), but we know there were many. The commanding officer told us to go back a few kilometres to an American field hospital where they would take care of us. He phoned ahead from the Jeep. They had the Nazis on the run. They were chasing the German army and couldn't stop now.

We were amazed to be so free, and we walked in the direction we were told. The highway was narrow and packed with lots of American military tanks and trucks with soldiers. A transport truck hit me, as I wasn't steady on my feet. I had stepped out a little more onto the road than I should have. I was taken to the military hospital unconscious and woke up two days later. When I opened my eyes, standing over me were two doctors and nurses shaking their heads. I weighed eighty pounds. It took a lot of effort to nurse me and the other two boys back to health. I will never forget the compassion and love I received in my recuperation.

I was shocked to learn that President Franklin D. Roosevelt had died April 12, 1945. I also learned that Vladimir (Ze'ev) Jabotinsky, the famed Zionist thinker, had died on August 4, 1940. Jabotinsky was the head of the Betar youth movement and I had heard him speak in 1938 when he was in Lodz. He appealed to the Jewish population to leave Poland and go to Palestine or any place outside Europe because he foresaw that staying in Europe would be a disaster. For his foresight, Jabotinsky was laughed at.

By the beginning of July 1945, I was more or less strong in body and mind. I started to think about my brother Ben. I missed him and wondered if he was alive. Had he survived the typhus? I asked permission to speak to the commanding officer. Permission was granted and he listened to me carefully as I told him I had left my only brother, who I thought might possibly be alive in the Dachau camp. I wanted to go back and search for him. Ben probably thought I was dead and would not know where to look for me. But the commanding officer wondered whether I was well enough to travel and take care of myself. My answer was, "Thank you so much. You did so much for me but I feel determined that it is time to find him, so I must be strong enough to do so." I received a document signed by the commanding officer with the seal of the American CIA stating who I was and asking the armed forces to assist me with accommodation, food and transport to my destination.

The trip took three days by military truck. I was dressed in a US military uniform because they did not have civilian clothing to give me, but I had no insignias. They told me I had had enough of prison clothing. The uniform was a little too big but I felt on top of the world in an American uniform in Germany. I was with American soldiers on German soil without the SS or Gestapo on my tail! The military personnel couldn't do enough for me. I am so very grateful to the United States Third Army for liberating me from the camps and giving me the opportunity to pursue a new life.

When I arrived at Dachau, just thirty kilometres from Munich, it looked different. It was already cleaner than I remembered. Outside the main gate, two American soldiers checked documents and questioned visitors. I showed my papers and the guard treated me with dignity. I told him whom I was looking for and that I had been a prisoner in this camp. He directed me to the office, where I repeated the information. They told me that Ben was in the town of Dachau, living in a small villa with three other men, and they gave me the address. I hitchhiked back to the town. When I stood outside the house, I thought, "I am liberated, well fed, healthy and going to meet my only known living relative. I have defeated Hitler and his band of murderers by surviving the Holocaust." I was pleased.

I knocked. A stranger opened the door and asked me what I wanted. I asked, "Does Ben Adler live here?" The man yelled behind him, "Ben, there is somebody to see you." It felt like I waited forever. At last Ben came out and shouted, "This is my kid brother! I thought he was dead!" Ben introduced me to his roommates, and that afternoon we had a celebration and a warm reunion.

Our lives began returning to normal after five years and six months of imprisonment. The best part was not getting up at five in the morning or standing in the rain and listening to the Nazis playing with our lives. American soldiers visited us to check if we were all right and needed anything. Ben received an old German motorcycle from some soldiers. To start it, he had to put it in gear, run beside it and then jump on.

One day, a CIA officer discussed with Ben the possibility of him becoming a translator for the agency, searching for Nazis in hiding. Ben spoke enough English to communicate. We were still tired and he explained that he would help in any way he could, but only in local situations, as he didn't want to travel. We were also offered the opportunity to go to the Far East to join American forces in Japan, after which we would become American citizens and settle in the United States once the war ended. But we declined that, too. We wanted to find our mother and Ben's wife, and to find out what had happened to Arthur. We registered with the Red Cross, the only way to find relatives.

At one point, we received news that our mother and Etta were alive and back in Poland! Ben said he was going home to investigate. How? I asked. He said if he had to, he would smuggle himself across the border. And that's exactly what he did. So I was all alone again, hoping he had gotten there safely and would return. In the meantime, I took a trip to Stuttgart to see old buddies from the Radom camp. They were happy to see me and asked me to stay. I told them that I had to go back to Dachau and wait for Ben to return from Poland. But when I got to Dachau, I was disappointed to hear that there was no news from Ben.

One morning, I came back from a walk and noticed a British military car outside our house, and I wondered who they had come to see. As I walked through the door, I saw the back of a military man in a British uniform. I knew instantly: it was my eldest brother, Arthur! Arthur had heard from my aunt in London through the Red Cross that we had survived and were living in Dachau. He had immediately asked for permission to travel to Germany to find us. We sat for hours telling each other about the missing six years of our lives and the loss of our father, Josef, our grandparents and so many of our relatives.

When Arthur left us in Lodz in November 1939, he tried to get to Romania and from there to England to join my mother's family. But when the Soviet army advanced from the east, he was caught and, suspected of being a German spy, sentenced to ten years' imprisonment in Siberia. He was sent to a work camp in the Ural Mountains, where the living conditions were rough, and at age twenty-two, he lost all his teeth because of poor nutrition. He was taken to a hospital and the female doctor took a liking to him. She gave him a job in the pharmacy, and soon the relationship became intimate. But because Arthur did not meet her expectations in that area, she sent him back to hard labour. In July 1941, the Polish government-in-exile in Britain arranged with the Soviet government to release thousands of Polish citizens, some of whom were eligible to join the British army. Arthur was part of this exchange. He was stationed in Ancona, Italy, and took part in the 1944 Battle of Monte Cassino.

Arthur was very disappointed at not being able to see Ben, who was still in Poland, and the news about our father and Josef devastated him. A week later, he had to go back to his unit. It was sad to say goodbye. The relationship between us had changed. We needed much more time to get back to the "kid brother–older brother" relationship. I was seventeen and he was a combat soldier. We wondered when we would see each other again. The consolation was that we were both alive and well, and could communicate with one another. He left me his address.

Now I was alone again with a lot of time on my hands, wondering about Ben and what to do next. At least I was not alone in the house at night. Using Ben's motorcycle, I went out and got to know a sixteen-year-old German girl. I always reminded her that I was Jewish and our relationship was only temporary, but I have nice memories of her.

After about one month, Ben returned from his trip — with no news about our mother and his wife, Etta. I told him all about Arthur. Ben was upset that he had not seen him but relieved that Arthur was alive and well. Life was calm and monotonous, but we needed the time to relax and unwind from the previous six years while we mourned the loss of family. Thoughts of the past were painful and unforgettable.

My relationship with Arthur was strained but something was pulling me to go to Italy to visit him. Before the war, he had been my role model, but now he was a stranger. I cannot explain why I had the urge to visit him, and I hated to leave Ben after what we had gone through. I chalk it up to destiny. Even today I think everything happened for a reason. Ben wasn't thrilled about my going to Italy but gave me his blessing.

Around the late fall of 1945, I hopped onto various freight trains and arrived in the city of Bolzano, in northern Italy. On several occasions, the Italians wanted to lynch me because I spoke German. After the country's occupation, they hated the Nazis as much as we did. One Italian gentleman felt sorry for me after I explained my situation and where I came from. He invited me to his apartment to meet his mother and family. This was my first encounter with Italian people. They were decent, warm folks, and even though I did not understand what he was telling them, I could read on their faces their sympathy and admiration. I had my first lesson in making spaghetti Italian-style on a long, eight-foot table to which a press was attached. The dough was fed into one end, while long strands of spaghetti were pulled out the other. The home-cooked meal tasted delicious and I felt alive.

The following morning I took a train to Ancona, a city on the east coast where Arthur was staying with his company. I arrived late in the afternoon and asked military personnel on the street where I could find his company. By the evening I came to the gate of the military camp where Arthur was staying. The guard asked me my business. He made a phone call. It took thirty minutes to locate Arthur and he came to the gate. What a surprise for him! He couldn't believe that I had travelled incognito between countries to see him. I was welcomed to stay with Arthur in the tent and was issued a British uniform but they wanted me to join the Jewish brigade, a group that was helping Jewish refugees enter Palestine. In the meantime, I lived a military life and was treated like a soldier. On leave days, we went to town with the other soldiers and I experienced many new things. I also got into trouble for not saluting a passing officer, which took a little time to explain. Once, Arthur and I were invited for dinner at the home of a prominent family he had met through their daughter. It was the first time I ate rabbit meat, which tasted like chicken, and I had a little too much wine. Arthur was embarrassed by my behaviour but the family had a good laugh from my antics.

Arthur worked distributing gas supplies to the division and became a translator between Polish officers and the British since he could speak school-level English. He was busy with his gasoline depot and I was free to roam around on my own. Over the next two weeks, the officers pressured Arthur to get me to join the unit, and he kept stalling. All I had to do was sign papers. But then, in early 1946, his orders came: the whole Polish division was sailing to England to be demobilized. Had I signed, I would have been shipped to England, too.

I intended to go back to Dachau but it was tougher because there were more restrictions on travel, so Arthur took me to Rome and introduced me to a few people, as he was sailing the next day. I was taken to Santa Cesarea, which is on the heel of the Italian boot, a nice small town where the Italian dictator Benito Mussolini had had his summer palace. I was assigned to a small villa four doors away from Mussolini's palace. A large part of the town was designated a Displaced Persons camp, run by the United Nations Relief and Rehabilitation Administration (UNRRA), an international relief agency that helped repatriate and support refugees who came under Allied control at war's end. I had to be there under an assumed name because I was there illegally, so, to get the food supplied by the UNRRA, I took the place of another boy who had been smuggled into Palestine by Aliyah Bet, the code name given to the group that organized illegal immigration to British Mandate Palestine. I assumed his identity until we decided what to do. I was leaning very strongly toward going to Palestine. I felt this was the time to do it.

I shared the villa with four others. We lived near the ocean, so swimming was just a short walk from our room. I became quite active in this kibbutz-style commune, which was populated by Jews from all over Europe, men and women ages seventeen to thirty-five. We had lectures, some schooling and learned the geography and history of Palestine. We played volleyball, Ping-Pong and football, and did a lot of swimming. I also joined a boxing team. We had dances, and although life was pleasant, I missed my family, especially Ben.

Since I participated in all activities and discussions, I was approached by a young man I had befriended named Katz. He wanted to discuss Israel and how to achieve the dream of having our own country. I told him that historically, the land belonged to us, and also that with the Balfour Declaration, the British government had supported our right to a homeland during World War I. Jewish soldiers had fought in both wars, helping the British to defeat Turkish rule in the first war and enlisting to fight the Nazis in the second, with many paying with their lives. He listened closely and left me with my own conclusion: that Palestine was the only place for me. A week went by and I was approached again and asked if I would sacrifice my freedom to fight in Palestine. My answer, without hesitation, was "Yes!" And that was the end of the meeting.

A few days went by and late one evening after supper, I was approached by another person, who instructed me to follow him. He led me to a completely dark room. At the far end was a table with a white tablecloth. I was instructed to approach the table, on which had been placed a hanukkiyah with candles burning, a Bible and a heavy 9 mm pistol. A voice in the darkness asked me if I was there of my own free will. My answer was yes. I was told to pick to up the Bible with my left hand (close to my heart) and the gun with my right and repeat after the voice. It was my swearing-in ceremony. I recognized only the three men who talked to me before the meeting — all the others were behind a curtain. I was congratulated for having become a member of the Irgun Zvai Le'umi, the National Military Organization. I considered them to be the freedom fighters that would liberate Palestine from the British occupation. Other people viewed their armed tactics differently and found some activities controversial.

In the spring of 1946, at eighteen years of age, I felt like a full-grown man who knew what was right and wrong, and I was willing to go to Palestine and contribute to the liberation of our long-lost country, fulfilling a promise I had made in the camps, lying in my bunk after work. The next day, I digested what I had experienced the previous night. I felt very proud of myself and thought, "This is my new life, and thank God I survived six years of misery, even though I lost part of my family." Life began to be exciting, but I still missed my brothers.

Over the next two weeks, it was hard work in the small forest in the nearby mountains. My training consisted of learning how to use a handgun, the Italian Beretta, and a rifle with a bayonet attached, like the ones carried by Italian police. We were buying them cheap. We also had American "Tommy guns." We had to learn to quickly take them apart and put them together with our eyes closed. The most intensive training was at night. We dressed in dark clothes and blackened our faces. I guess that this was training for future exercises in Israel. When I finished my training, I received a yellow folder containing papers written in Hebrew, a passport-sized photograph of Vladimir Jabotinsky and a commendation for achievements and discipline. I also received a German automatic 9 mm pistol. The Germans called it a Parabellum — it was big and heavy and hard to conceal.

My first assignment was to rent a bicycle and deliver printed leaflets to a sister kibbutz thirty kilometres away. There were small towns every twenty to thirty kilometres in this part of southern Italy, a region called Puglia. The nearest big city was Lecce and after that, a larger one, Bari. Our next assignment was to paint protest slogans on the British occupation's military equipment.

We did a lot of different things to gain training and experience in preparation for the day we would be allowed to go to Israel legally and fight for our country. In the meantime, our help was needed in Italy and so we followed orders just like a regular army would. A lot of people then, as now, considered us not as freedom fighters but as terrorists. Even so, it was an exciting and beautiful life I was living after what I had gone through.

The Decision

My superiors, Jews who had come from Palestine to Italy illegally, considered sending me to Palestine via Aliyah Bet but decided to do that at a later date. They said I was more useful and needed in Santa Cesarea. I was a little disappointed not to be going to Palestine, but I had to follow orders and I was satisfied that what I was doing was important. I travelled the length of Italy in a British uniform, but I did not dare wear the military insignia. I did not need to be recognized by the Italians as a soldier of the occupation forces, but had the British caught me, it would have meant prison for impersonating a soldier.

On one of my trips south by train, we stopped in the port city of Bari. At the station the conductor asked for tickets and travel documents, which I did not have. When he came to me, I produced that yellow file folder with Jabotinsky's photograph on the front page. The conductor looked at it from all sides and since it was in Hebrew and he couldn't read it, I kept telling him, in Italian, "Secret, secret." He looked at the picture and asked who it was. My answer came fast: "Mr. Truman." He looked at me, saluted and walked away. I was sweating and shaking! If he had called the British military police, I would probably have been thrown in jail.

Our assignment was to take illegal travellers out by rubber pontoons to the ships waiting a few kilometres offshore. We guarded the beaches and boats with Tommy guns. Many times, I wondered how we would react if the British soldiers interfered. Many young Jewish officers who had deserted the Soviet army in Austria, Hungary and Romania were brought to us to be shipped to Palestine. Some of the ships were caught by the British in their blockade of Palestine and shipped to Cyprus. What had happened to the British promise of accepting Jewish war refugees?

At some point, I received a letter from Stockholm, Sweden, with a picture of my mother, Ben and Etta. They had gotten my address from Arthur. I was so thrilled to learn that my mother and Ben's wife had survived, and that Ben was with them. I found out that the Swedish government had been responsible for my mother's liberation. Representatives from Sweden's Red Cross had been negotiating with Heinrich Himmler since February 1945 to release Scandinavian prisoners, as well as prisoners of other nationalities, from Germany. By April 1945, they managed to also free one thousand Jewish women from Ravensbrück, a camp for women only, where my mother and sister-in-law were imprisoned. My mother and sister-in-law had been shipped there after being in Auschwitz for a few months. When they arrived in Sweden, the Swedish people nursed them back to health and placed them in jobs.

My mother and Etta were working in a hospital. When they got settled, they asked if they could bring Ben and me to Sweden, but since I was not in Germany, Ben went on his own. All the communications had begun through my aunt's family with help from the Red Cross. I kept receiving letters from my mother on a regular basis and from Arthur in London. He was already a civilian. The pressure was on for me to come to Stockholm to be reunited with everyone. I had to make a serious decision between staying and working to contribute to our cause, or being reunited with my surviving family. It was not easy and I stalled as much as I could before deciding to stay where I was.

I felt that my group was doing a lot of good by sending young, healthy people to Palestine. In 1946, we dispatched a ship of refugees to Palestine, but the British turned it back to the detention camp in Cyprus. Amid our outcries and pain, the Irgun headquarters in Israel issued an order to blow up the British Embassy in Rome. On October 31, 1946, late in the afternoon, the embassy received leaflets advising its staff to leave the building immediately. The building was emptied in a few minutes and traffic was stopped. The British Embassy was bombed, and three people were injured. Experienced people had been brought in for the operation, and I was not involved. The most important thing was that no human life was lost, and we apologized to the Italian authorities.

In 1947, orders arrived that our camp was to be closed and we would be moved out to the city of Bari, to a much bigger Displaced Persons camp. After that, the decision on what to do with the refugees would be made. Some applied to go to the United States, others to Australia. Everybody had relatives somewhere. On arrival at the new location, I was unhappy — it was harder to be active behind fences and without the ocean nearby.

At nineteen years old, I resolved that I wouldn't spend my time on Cyprus behind barbed wire in a camp again. All such camps, I felt, deprived one of freedom. I informed my superiors and they did not hold it against me, especially as I was going to be reunited with my mother. They told me I would be missed and hoped to meet me someday again in a free Israel. My love for my mother and anticipation at being reunited with Ben took precedence above all.

Near the end of 1947, I corresponded with my family in Stockholm and informed them that I would join them. The wheels were set in motion to get me a visa and a job. Ben was working in a factory producing instruments for airplanes and submarines and he got me a job there. My mother applied for a visa for me on humanitarian grounds and because I had employment. I received a letter from the Swedish embassy in Rome saying a visa was waiting for me and asking me to come for an interview. At the embassy it was explained to me that I needed a valid passport and that since I was born in Po-

land, I should go to the Polish embassy for one. There, an officer interviewed me and actually suggested that I return to Poland, as young
men were needed there to rebuild the country! I explained to him
that I had been interned in the Nazi camps and wanted to reunite
with my family, but he had a one-track mind. Poland was by then a
communist country and we got into a very heated discussion about
freedom and democracy. He said I was on Polish soil and could be
arrested. I agreed with him. He stared at me, then excused himself
and walked out to an adjoining office. As soon as he was gone, I
walked out the other way, quickly.

After deliberating, I decided to go to the Red Cross for help. The
next day, I went to the International Red Cross in Rome and told
them about the Polish embassy and being rejected for a passport because of my democratic views, and that I had a visa waiting for me at
the Swedish embassy. In one hour I was given a "Stateless Passport"
with my picture on it. Now I was a stateless person with no country
— it felt like being an orphan. Back I went to the Swedish embassy,
where they had never seen such a document. It had a white cover,
which gave it an unusual look, and included an explanation that I
was without citizenship of any country, but that the International Red
Cross vouched for me. Now I had all the necessary documents but no
money for the trip.

Since the UNRRA had supported me in the DP camps, I told them
my predicament and they bought me a plane ticket from Rome to
Stockholm. The journey, my first on an airplane, took nine hours.
Ben picked me up at the airport in Stockholm and we had an incred-
ible reunion. My mother, however, was not there because she had just
been granted a visa to London, England, to visit her sister, whom she
had not seen for thirty-eight years. Ben's wife, Etta, was home waiting
for us with their newborn baby girl, Eva. What a wonderful surprise!
After a few weeks, my mother returned to Stockholm. We were the
best of friends, and we had a tearful, joyous reunion.

Building a New Life

On my arrival, the first thing Ben and Etta did was to take me to get civilian clothes and rent me a room nearby. We lived in the suburb of Råsunda, a thirty-minute bike ride from Stockholm.

I started working with Ben at the factory, which produced instruments for aircrafts, submarines and other major transport vehicles. We all had to wear white coats, laboratory style. My job was to test the instruments before shipping. My income was decent and the job was unionized. I worked from 7:00 a.m. to 3:00 p.m. and signed up for school from 5:00 p.m. to 10:00 p.m. at the Stockholm Technical Institute. On the weekends I was tutored in mathematics. My aim was to be a bridge and highway engineer. At the technical college, I met up again with the younger Zuckerman brother, from the Radom camp. He was living in Stockholm with his older brother, and I was so glad to know they had both survived the war. I eventually quit my studies because it was too hard to go to work and school and also have a social life. I was hungry for a social life — my precious teenage years had been stolen from me and I could not get them back no matter how hard I tried.

I learned Swedish quickly; by now, I could communicate in Polish, Yiddish, Hebrew, German, Italian and Swedish. I began making friends among other expatriates, quite a few of whom were from Denmark and Norway, and I found a Betar office in Stockholm run by a young man from Finland. We became friends and I received the key to the premises. I also joined the Swedish B'nai Brith, which was run by a middle-aged Swede. Jewish life in Stockholm was quite assimilated but the Jewish teenagers did not ignore being Jewish. I was busy in all directions and made up for lost time socially. I was happy and popular, although it was hard to shake off suspicions and the feeling of always needing to be on my guard. I wanted so badly to blend in. I felt I deserved all the fun that life had to offer as a reward for having beaten the Nazis by surviving.

The young ladies I met were sympathetic to me and seemed to find my accent amusing. And when the news spread that my mother and brother lived in the suburbs of Stockholm and that I had just arrived from Italy, it didn't take long before phone calls and letters arrived from various Jewish women. From Radom, women survivors outnumbered the men, and many were looking for husbands. On one occasion, I received a phone call from Zosia, the young woman who had been my first "puppy love" at school in Lublin. She lived several hundred kilometres away. I asked her to come for a visit and said she could stay with Ben and Etta. She took my invitation seriously and came for two weeks, and we had a really nice time. I got a little serious about her and we spoke on the phone quite often after she returned home. She was ready to get married but I got cold feet. I was sorry to break her heart, but I was only nineteen years old and I felt that my future was so uncertain.

Stockholm is a beautiful city with a 750-year history. There were so many places to see, and I really enjoyed being there. The city is built on small islands with many bridges. It was especially enjoyable on weekends, visiting museums, parks and castles. In the summer, the days are so long that by mid-June the daylight lasts nearly twenty hours. On summer weekends, I would go to the famous Tivoli amusement park in Stora Scenen, where dances and concerts were held. I spent many memorable evenings there with my two buddies, Kuba Hanovitz and Eddie Volkman. My two friends and I were inseparable; we were the same age and everybody called us the Three

Musketeers. Eddie had spent several years in Mauthausen concentration camp and Kuba had been a partisan in eastern Poland. Eddie eventually immigrated to New York; Kuba remained in Stockholm.

~

In 1948, when Israel declared its independence and was backed by the United Nations, Arab nations attacked the new state on several fronts, armed with the weapons of the departing British occupiers who had confiscated guns from Jewish settlers. The little country was left to defend itself any way it could. With God's help and some friendly countries, Israel defeated all the Arab armies.

On Independence Day, May 14, 1948, an office was opened in Stockholm for recruiting volunteers for the Israel Defense Forces (IDF). I was ready to go but my mother was in tears and pressured me not to, saying Arthur was in London, Ben in Canada and after finding me, she couldn't bear to part with me. So, I decided to stay with my mother in Stockholm. It was hard to choose between love and responsibility to my mother and a country I loved. The situation was like the one in Italy, where I had been torn in different directions.

Later that year Arthur came for a visit to meet his new sister-in-law and newborn niece. He hadn't seen Ben since 1939, so we had a lot to catch up on. We missed our father and Josef, but our lives had to go on. In 1948, Ben and his family received a visa to go to Canada. My sister-in-law had an uncle living in Toronto and he wanted them to settle in Canada. I told them to go and that I would eventually join them. In Europe, the past felt too close. We feared another war, what with the Cold War going on. At least Canada was far away, and it felt safe at the time.

In 1949, Arthur and my mother wanted to introduce me to our families in England. Arthur became engaged to a young lady named Jackie Unger and I was invited to come to the party. Arthur's future father-in-law had arranged for a tourist visa for me from the British embassy in Stockholm, and I then presented myself at the embassy with my International Red Cross passport. The officer took a look at my passport and said, rudely, that he could not stamp a visa onto this type of document. I responded by saying, "If the Swedish government accepted this document and granted me a visa, what makes you that much better?" I walked out.

I wrote to Arthur about the episode at the embassy and told him I couldn't attend his engagement party. He was upset and told Jackie's father, who had arranged the visa for me. Mr. Unger was chief architect for the City of London, and he had received many decorations from the King for the defence of London. He made one phone call to the Home Office department and a few days later I received a call from the embassy. I walked in there with my passport in hand and was directed to another officer who apologized and stamped the visa immediately, as the previous officer looked on, wondering what had happened!

My London visit was most enjoyable. I met my aunt, uncle and all the cousins. It was a new experience to see the luxurious lives my cousins had. It took me back to my childhood. I went downtown by subway and visited the Tower of London and all the museums. London became one of my favourite cities.

~

The Jewish Federation in Stockholm arranged many programs and through one in July 1950 I met my wife, Ruth Elias. She had come to Stockholm as a child via the Kindertransport, a rescue operation that brought thousands of Jewish refugee children out of Nazi Germany between 1938 and 1940. Her parents had been sent to the Theresienstadt ghetto and camp. Her mother survived but her father was later shipped to Auschwitz-Birkenau, where he perished.

Ruth had an interesting story to tell. As a young child she had been separated from her parents and sent to a strange country with a strange language; however, it was much safer to be in a neutral country like Sweden than in one under the Nazi occupation.

In September 1950, Ruth and I went to London for Arthur and Jackie's wedding. One day, I invited Ruth to come with me on an outing on a motorbike. While riding, I said to her, "If you won't marry me, I will crash the bike!" I felt her hands tighten around my hips. She agreed. At Arthur's wedding party, Ruth and I became engaged.

On December 17, 1950, Ruth and I got married in Stockholm. After living with my mother for a short time, we got an apartment in a new building in the suburbs. It was the perfect place to raise a child.

Ruth was managing the office of a company manufacturing cosmetics and I found a job in the fur business, which was very big in Sweden. I landed a job in the largest company in Stockholm as a trainee dealing in skins only. It takes years to learn the qualities, colour and value of furs but as I worked in the fur industry, gaining experience, I soon mastered the skills to become an expert on certain types of furs. The industry was lucrative.

I still talked about leaving Europe, even though we had many friends and Ruth's mother, Elizabeth, and my mother did not want us to leave. I had lost confidence in the security of Europe, a place where two world wars had begun. North America looked far enough from all the evil. Ben and Etta were by then in Toronto and asked us to come over and settle there. One day, we were invited to a party where we saw a couple of Ruth's old friends, the Stenges. Margrit and Stefan had immigrated to Canada in 1949 and were living in Montreal. They told us how nice and peaceful it was there. That night, I got a bug in my head about moving to Canada.

In 1951, I asked Ben to arrange the immigration papers for us; we intended to bring our mothers over, too, within a relatively short time. Immigration to Canada at that time was not easy unless you were a refugee, which we weren't any longer. Ben arranged all the proper immigration papers and guarantees stating we wouldn't be a burden on the Canadian government. By the end of 1951 we got the visas, but we first had to go to a Canadian doctor for a physical and mental examination. We also had to produce papers from the local and provincial police stating that we were decent people and attesting to our honesty of character. We passed almost all the examinations, except the Canadian doctor told me I had scar tissue on my right lung and had to be under observation for a year before I could get the visa. What a disappointment! I felt humiliated. It seemed as though immigration to Canada was out for the time being and I would have to accept it. But something made me decide to have myself checked out by a local doctor. I consulted two doctors and both confirmed I was in excellent health. Stockholm had excellent lung and internal medicine specialists, and they explained that the tissue on my right lung was a scar dating either to birth or to a bad cold in the camps during the war. The assessments by the two specialists made me feel strong and healthy. I told Ruth that we should forget about Canada and instead build a life in Sweden. And we did.

~

On September 17, 1953, my son, Barry, was born. It was an exciting day for the two grandmothers and Ruth and me. At twenty-five, I became a father as well as a Swedish citizen, and I was confident that my life was turning around. Sweden did not confer citizenship easily. I was allowed to join the Swedish armed forces for two years. In Sweden, when you are in the army, the government supports the family and provides medical benefits. I was proud to belong to such a country.

Sometimes I felt like a newborn, but the nightmares were stubborn. I don't know how other survivors coped with their experiences; for me it was still too fresh. The days were all right but at night, the fear haunted me. Knowing I had Ruth and the baby and, of course, our mothers and brothers, helped to ease the pain.

In 1954, I received an exciting and rewarding offer from a fur company in the city of Malmö, in the southern part of Sweden across the channel from Copenhagen. I was tempted to accept it but I still had to go to the military for eighteen months and I was debating once again about moving to Canada. The Korean War had ended recently, the

Cold War was still going on, and it felt to me as though if there were going to be another war, it would start in Europe. I didn't want that for my family. Our visas were still active, and I had the doctors' notes proving I was healthy. Weighing all the plusses and minuses, we made the decision to go to Canada. I wrote to the Swedish government for permission to leave the country and it was granted on condition that if I ever returned, I would have to do military service.

We sold our apartment and left Sweden for England in October 1954, booking our trip to Quebec City via England. This time we were travelling not as refugees but as immigrants paying our own way. We even booked first-class tickets on the train from Quebec City to Montreal. Ben insisted on picking us up by car in Montreal.

We stayed with Arthur and Jackie in London for one week while we showed off our new baby boy to the family there. We had an excellent week with my brother and spent a lot of time with my cousins, aunt and uncle.

Hurricane Hazel slammed North America in October 1954, making the seas rocky and hazardous on the RMS *Scythia*. Ruth is a poor traveller and was seasick through the whole crossing. The baby and I, on the other hand, had a fine time. I walked, played Ping-Pong and talked with other passengers, but it was still a long eight-day trip on an old ship. We arrived in Quebec City and after clearing customs, got on the first-class train to Montreal. It was a comfortable and enjoyable trip and Ruth finally started to feel better.

In the evening, when the conductor announced that the next stop was Montreal, we left the train, but we found ourselves standing in the middle of nowhere, near a small hut with the lights of the city in the distance. I asked myself, Is this Montreal? There we were, standing with a baby and our luggage, without a soul around. In the hut was a person selling tickets and after a long discussion and explanation, we realized we were in a suburb. We called a taxi and arrived in Montreal late at night. Ben, who had driven from Toronto to meet us, had been waiting at the station, and, disappointed when we didn't

arrive, had left. Luckily, he'd had a feeling that he had missed us earlier and had come back.

That night we stayed with friends and in the morning we started
out by car on the old Highway 2 to our new life in Toronto. We stayed
with Ben for six weeks in a small house and soon came to the conclusion that we had to get our own apartment. I had gotten work in
a chesterfield company, and we were able to rent a small apartment
behind a store on Eglinton Avenue West.

Canada, and Toronto, was a very important centre in the fur business and I knocked on many doors for a job. I had the credentials but
either I was over-qualified or the companies were too small to support what I had to offer. I took what I could find to make a living, as
I did not want to use up my savings. Ruth was unhappy and wanted
to return to Sweden. As I took on different jobs, it crossed my mind,
as well, to go back to Sweden, where we had been stable and enjoyed
all the conveniences of modern life in the fifties. Now we were strug-
gling, not used to these difficult living conditions. But I hoped for a
new and safe future and that kept me going. I did not give up. I would
say that as long as we had hope there was a chance, but at times, I
thought that maybe I was kidding myself. My biggest disappointment
was when I was called a "Greenie," a derogatory word for newcomers.

The best part of that time was when Ben would pick us up on
Friday afternoons to spend the weekend with them in his backyard.
Ben's one-year-old twins, Marc and Francis, played with my son and
we had a pleasant time. The twins and Barry grew up like siblings.
Ruth and Etta, Ben's wife, became close, like sisters.

At last, after two years, I landed a job in the fur business at a small
manufacturer of fine quality furs that had a very good reputation.
Even if over-qualified and underpaid, at least I was in the business.
And it paid off. Toronto was a small city then and news about me
spread fast in the industry.

In the mid-1950s Ben purchased a large home and built a base-
ment apartment, which we moved into. After two years of living with

my brother, we purchased a small bungalow. Offers for my services came in fast and I was able to increase my income. I was offered an executive position by one of the biggest manufacturers of mink coats and other fur garments and I took it. I loved my job. I had big responsibilities and a variety of duties. My income increased two-and-a-half-fold. I proved that despite hardships after arriving in a new country, once you develop a reputation, you can dictate your terms.

On July 10, 1958, my baby girl, Rose, was born and I felt like I had won the lottery. In a short time, I purchased a large, new home in a subdivision. Most of my neighbours were professionals and we became good friends; we also joined a synagogue and B'nai Brith, in which Ruth and I became very active. We soon managed to bring my mother-in-law and my mother to Canada.

In 1959, I got my big break: I received a call for an interview from an American firm that supplied furs to the manufacturers. It was headquartered in Chicago and had offices all over the world. The Toronto manager was being transferred to Montreal and they were looking for someone to take his place. After a short interview, I got the job running a multi-million dollar operation. My name became well known and respected in the industry, and I was invited to join the Fur Association's board of directors. I was thirty-one years old and had become part of the decision-making process on how much credit to extend to each manufacturer according to the financial statement they supplied us, much like how a bank works. I felt I had achieved some stature and prestige in the industry.

I worked hard during the busy seasons but in the summer I had more time to spend with my family and newly acquired friends. My next-door neighbour had just graduated from law school and he was a three-handicap golfer. He introduced me to golf and I joined the Richmond Hill Golf and Country Club. I caught the golf bug and entertained my clients on the course. I never became a great golfer, but I still love it and play a decent game. Our social life grew rich in friends and neighbours, but even though life was exciting, I still had nightmares about the past, an issue that would stay with me for the rest of my life.

In B'nai Brith, Ruth became president of her chapter and I was nominated for president the same year. I had to decline. Between having small children and my obligation to the company, I decided to wait until the next year. It would have been too hard to have Ruth and me as president at the same time. We would be away from the children too often. I went through every position — aside from recording secretary because, even though I had taken English classes, my English was not perfect — and stayed as vice-president for three years. But when the time came that I could have taken on the presidency, I was passed over. That upset me. After fifteen years as a member, I resigned. I have received many awards from B'nai Brith in Washington and Toronto for bringing in the most members and for many other achievements. Resigning from B'nai Brith did not affect our social life and I found new interests, joining a Masonic Lodge and graduating into a Shriner.

It was a privilege and an honour to join the Masonic Lodge — after I was investigated and approved, I spent thirty-eight years as a member in good standing. In my first year I was in line to eventually become Master of the Lodge, a position that usually takes up to ten years to achieve. I served for three years in the officers' line and then had to give it up because I travelled a lot in my business, so my time was limited, and also, the old English used by the Masonry was too difficult for me to remember. Even though I stepped out from the officers' line, I still participate in all the parades as much as my time permits.

In the late 1970s, Israeli Prime Minister Menachem Begin visited Toronto on an Israel Bonds drive. I was introduced to him by his security detail, some of whom I knew from my years in Italy. They had recognized me as I entered the temple where Begin was speaking. Begin asked me what I was doing in Canada. I told him it was a long story and that he didn't have the time for it. We had a nice talk and I felt privileged to meet him. He was one of my heroes, may he rest in peace. My other hero is former Israeli prime minister Ariel Sharon, who died in 2014. We are missing leaders like those two, especially now with the dangers posed by Iran. But it is my opinion that Iran will end up as all our enemies have: defeated.

Just as the fur industry took on a new way of doing business, I decided to branch off on my own and become an agent. My company, however, wouldn't let me quit and proposed a new deal: I would continue to represent them in Toronto and be a free agent, going to all the fur sales in Montreal, North Bay, Edmonton, New York and Europe. I could purchase furs for my European customers and still be in charge of the company's office in Toronto. This appealed to me and worked out well financially.

My first trip overseas was to West Berlin. I felt strange, especially when I saw German police patrolling the aircraft. My heart started to race until I controlled my thoughts and told myself, Amek, you are here, healthy and wealthy. Ignore them. You won the battle against the Nazis. Still, it felt odd being in Berlin, the capital, where all the evil had begun. At the same time, I felt proud staying at the fancy Hilton Hotel, built by Americans, possibly being served by the descendants of people who had wanted to remove Jews from earth. My life had become meaningful and rich.

I also flew to London, Stockholm, Copenhagen, West Berlin, Amsterdam and Oslo twice a year to sell my clients Canadian furs and purchase European furs for Canadian clients. Often, I flew to Montreal and our central office in Chicago. I imported European furs for Canada and exported Canadian furs to Europe until a French actress stepped in. In the late 1970s, Brigitte Bardot started campaigning against the wearing of fur and killing of seals. As a result, the fur industry started to go downhill and I decided it was time to get out. It was a hard decision. The industry had been good to me and my family and I had liked the excitement.

What to do now, I asked myself? I still had teenagers at home and had to earn a living. Offers and suggestions came in but nothing appealed to me. Then, in the early 1980s, I was introduced to a display company in Toronto that employed four salespeople. They gave me national clients like Eaton's and the Hudson's Bay Company. This was a period when new shopping malls were sprouting up all over Canada. About eight major shopping malls were built in Toronto alone. The Bay and Eaton's kept me hopping busy in every province. Eaton's main store was being built on Yonge Street and The Bay's on Bloor Street East. I was doing so well and those companies liked to do business with me.

I liked what I was doing — I had the freedom to come and go as I pleased. The company purchased a new car for me and gave me an unlimited expense account. In the meantime, I was called by Ontario Store Fixtures to take over their sales department for Canada. I was aware of their internal problems and declined. A year later, the company declared bankruptcy.

After two years of conflicts with my company's sales manager, I decided to leave. The owner was in tears and promised me tons of advantages if I stayed, but I had had enough. A week or so later, we were invited to a friend's barbeque, where I met the owner of a newly formed jewellery manufacturer. He had heard about me from mutual friends and offered me a sales position for Ontario and the four Atlantic provinces. I told him I knew nothing about jewellery, but he said I would learn on the job and that diamonds were graded like furs — by colour, size, quality and clarity. I spent two weeks in the factory and learned the basics so I wouldn't get lost in conversation with a client.

In my second career, I spent twenty-one years with this company and did well, to the point that I joined the most productive and high-earning sales representatives. I got involved with the Canadian Jewellers Association and, in 1989, was elected its president. As in the fur industry, I built an excellent name and reputation in the jewellery business, which introduced me to a big part of Canada.

I enjoyed living in Toronto, even though I never stopped think-ing about my six years of misery during the Nazi era. I never forgot where I came from and the suffering I had gone through during the war. My scars did not heal the same way as a cut on the finger. As much as I gave love to my immediate family, I concede that I had lin-gering issues.

Speaking Out

In 1994, I lost my beloved mother. I knew she wouldn't be here for-ever, but it was a reminder again of losing a loved one. I was grateful for her ninety-four years and that she had her full mental faculties to her last days.

Three years later, in 1997, I was approached by director Steven Spielberg's Survivors of the Shoah Visual History Foundation to video my experience for its archives in Los Angeles. Spielberg's film *Schindler's List*, which had been released in 1993, led to the establish-ment of the foundation. In my opinion, *Schindler's List* is the most realistic of all the movies on the subject of the Holocaust. It was only after the film's release that I decided to speak out as a survivor and get involved in Holocaust education by telling my story.

After I retired, I wanted to go to Israel and work for the army or as a chaperone with the March of the Living. In 2006 I applied and was accepted for both; I chose to go with the March as a survivor and tell the students my stories. The March did a lot for me and I am grateful for the opportunity to recount my experiences. Talking about what had happened to me in Poland and Germany released a weight that I had carried on my shoulders for over sixty years. We survivors carry a lot of such painful memories, which will stay with us to the end of our days.

Before the trip, my daughter wrote a beautiful letter for me to read on the plane.

April 22, 2006

Dad,

In my family, I started a tradition when the kids were little that when they were going to camp, I would write them a bus letter. Now, traditionally, our family always writes each other plane or bus letters. These letters are to be opened up when on the plane or bus in the beginning of the trip. So, here is your first plane letter.

Dear Dad,

Even though I am not sitting beside you right now, I am with you full heart and soul. I am shepping such nachas [getting such pride] *from you. We have had such a wonderful father/daughter relationship from the day we came into each other's lives. This trip, and these past few months preparing for it, I have watched you grow and I have watched you become a person of even greater strength than I have ever seen before. There are so many stages to life, God intends so many things for us as individuals and as families and friends that, if we are lucky, we develop and grow and become more knowledgeable in all aspects of our life. Then, some days, God puts in front of us situations where we have to rise to awareness of what is expected of us on our journey. I know that many times you have been put in these situations — loss of family; loss of home life; starting over in business; financial, emotional, physical traumas. You do have a story. But through it all, you have always come out shining, loving and nurturing as a man, a person, a husband, a father, a brother, a son, a friend and of course as a grandfather. This moment, this trip represents all of this. God has offered you a moment in time to share and as well to go back to Poland where it all started. As you go forward on this journey remember that you are a wonderful person, and I hope you shep your own nachas from your life to date.*

I want you to know that I am very proud to be your daughter, and I am so excited for you to be going on this journey. I pray that you and the others on your trip will enjoy each other's energies and grow in wisdom, friendship and peace together.

We will be here waiting for your return. I will see you like Moses, when he came down the mountain after speaking with God; you will share that wisdom on this trip.

I also want to let you know that your mother will be with you, protecting you on this journey. She loves you and is proud of you, as we all are.

Enjoy, be happy and stay safe.

All my love, your daughter,

Rose

The trip back to my wartime past was hard to make. I visited places where, if the ground could talk and tell the world what the Nazis did, the deniers of the Holocaust would be silent forever. The following year, I was invited again to go on the March of the Living and tell my life story. I accepted the assignment with pride. The second time turned out to be harder than the first. On the first trip I was tense and held back, not wanting to show the students my pain. I was more relaxed the second time, but it hurt more remembering. The memories were twice as hard to reveal without breaking down, so I decided not to go again.

But in late summer 2007, when recruiting time came about, I had lunch with Sherri Rotstein, who was in charge of the March and one of my favourite people, and David, who was in charge of security. They asked me if I would go on the 2008 March of the Living. When I declined, there was obvious disappointment on their faces. We had a long discussion on why they felt I should go, and by the end of the lunch, I had agreed to do the March again. I came to see the March as a sign for me to tell the next generation what we went through during the six years of Nazi occupation.

Following that, I was sent by UJA Federation's Neuberger Holocaust Education Centre to a variety of non-Jewish schools to talk about the Holocaust. I also was invited to speak to two classes at my grandson's school in Coral Springs, Florida. We left on the March of the Living on April 28, 2008, with 133 young students, twelve chaperones, two administrators and three survivors. I was glad I had changed my mind.

In Warsaw we went directly by bus to the Okopowa Street Jewish Cemetery, also known as the Gęsia Cemetery, for a memorial service. The next morning, we travelled to Tykocin, a small town where 2,500 Jews once lived. In the summer of 1941, the Nazis took them to the Łopuchowo forest, outside the town, where they were all executed in mass graves. We had a memorial service there. The same day, we stopped in the small town of Jedwabne, where at least 350 Jews were locked in a barn, which was then set on fire by Polish residents in July 1941. The Polish government has since issued an official apology for the pogrom and made a shrine on the location.

Our next stop was Treblinka, the death camp, which was built only for that one purpose. We had a memorial service there and I found the memorial stone in the name of the city of Radom, my father's birthplace, where all his relatives were murdered. After a hard, sorrowful day, we departed for Warsaw for dinner and debriefing in the evening. There were several hundred teenagers from all over the world in attendance.

The next morning, we departed by bus to Auschwitz, where we visited the museum. The students were exposed to the horrors of the camp and it was an emotional and disturbing day. The next day, May 1, we returned to Auschwitz for Yom HaShoah, Holocaust Memorial Day, and for the International March of the Living from Auschwitz to Birkenau, with 11,000 participants from all over the world.

The March is done in silence, with arms linked, and we slowly walk the three kilometres from Auschwitz to Birkenau. Arriving in Birkenau is a very dramatic experience, no matter how many times

I participate. Several of the students and chaperones were emotional and needed support. The three-kilometre march is the main purpose of the trip, meant to recreate the march Nazi victims were forced to make from Auschwitz to Birkenau. The fleeing Nazis destroyed the crematoria at Birkenau and the rubble is maintained as a shrine. All 11,000 of us held a memorial service, with speeches by dignitaries from Israel and Poland. The weather did not cooperate as in previous years. Nature was empathizing with us and it rained, as though the heavens themselves cried. What an emotional day, sitting on the wet grass and listening to the commander of Israel's military defences and other dignitaries in the place where just sixty years earlier, Jews were being slaughtered. Even thinking about those days makes me shiver. I feel blessed to be alive and to be able to talk about it.

After leaving Auschwitz we travelled to Tarnów, a small town where we visited a memorial site that marked all that was left of a synagogue and a community of Jews. We stayed that night in Tarnów for dinner and a well-deserved rest. The next day we departed for Bełżec, which is in the middle of nowhere. This camp was built for the purpose of murdering Jews in the most barbaric way.

Later the same day we arrived at Lublin, my birthplace, to stay over the weekend and visit the great yeshiva and the Majdanek concentration camp, only a few kilometres from the city. In addition to the crematorium and gas chambers, we saw a mountain of ashes under a dome, preserved with chemicals to last forever as a memorial. Next to it are mass graves into which the dead were thrown the same day they arrived. Majdanek, in my opinion, is today the holiest of shrines for Jews. Everything is operational and visibly intact. I have two places to mourn: Treblinka, the burial place of my father's relatives from Radom, and Majdanek, where relatives from my mother's side, from Lublin, perished.

We returned to Warsaw for religious services and dinner and then departed to Israel for a well-deserved change of surroundings. I can't speak for the other survivors, but leaving Poland for Israel felt like substituting Hell for Heaven. It is hard to describe our mood upon arriving in Israel, where we were about to celebrate sixty years of independence. I felt like I was on top of the world.

After touring Jerusalem's Old City, we travelled to the northern borders with Syria and Lebanon, and to the south, where we had dinner with Bedouins in a desert camp. We attended the memorial for the fallen soldiers of Israel, on a day known as Yom HaZikaron. The most dramatic place, in my opinion, was the cemetery atop Mount Herzl where the young defenders of Israel are laid to rest, and of course Yad Vashem, the Holocaust memorial and museum. We also attended a celebration for Yom Ha'atzmaut, the birth of Israel.

On the flight home, I went through the three March of the Living trips I had made and concluded that I was glad I made them. Even though they had caused much discomfort and triggered horrible memories, which I am still trying to forget, I feel they were worth it. I have been told by chaperones that from the few marches I missed, the kids could hardly wait to come back to see me. It is great to know that I made a positive impression on the students. That is what all we survivors try to do: tell our history.

~

Back in the late 1970s, I had happened to meet the Post Commander of the Toronto post of the Jewish War Veterans of Canada, and as we spoke I told him I'd been involved with the Israeli Irgun in Italy between 1945 and 1947. The Post Commander qualified me as military personnel and strongly suggested I join the Jewish War Veterans in Toronto. I did join in 1980 and I was very proud of serving the organization; immodestly, I was invited to serve on the Board of Directors and appointed to be chairman of membership. Eventually, I became vice-president.

The organization went through a lot of changes and hardships, and when we faced financial issues I was able to secure for us new office space at the UJA Federation of Toronto in 1995. Our main objective became to build a monument to honour the Jewish fallen soldiers in the Canadian armed forces during both world wars and the Korean War. I made a presentation to the federation, where I broached the idea of building a monument and putting the names of all the Canadian Jews who had served on one side and the ones who did not come back alive on the other side, with flags and insignias of branches that would recognize major donors. The Federation suggested a number of different places for the monument, none of which I was satisfied with. On many occasions I demanded the respect and honour we owed to the armed forces, and finally they asked me where I wanted the monument to be. I picked a prime space — on the grounds of UJA Federation's Sherman Campus — and now we have a beautiful monument with Canadian and Israeli flags flying across from the Toronto Federation.

On November 11, 2011, at 11:00 a.m., the monument was unveiled, with the minister of defence from Ottawa in attendance, along with veterans and hundreds of others. We all felt so proud.

Epilogue

It took me three years to write these pages. It was hard for me to sit down and put my memories on paper. There were times I stayed away from the manuscript for weeks and months because more than two to three hours at a time were already too much.

Along with this memoir, my two-and-a-half-hour videotape made for the USC Shoah Foundation, and four years of travelling with the March of the Living — I decided to go again in 2009 but refused after that, as I couldn't see myself facing those horrible places one more time — I feel I will be leaving enough history behind for future generations of Jews to read and, I hope, not allow this to happen again under any circumstances.

As a survivor, I never wanted sympathy from anybody. Since I began with the March of Living, I feel that survivors have earned more respect from Jews and from some Christians. Time is taking its toll and there are fewer of us each year.

When my grandson Evan was studying at the University of British Columbia, Kelowna Campus, he asked me about whether I felt that being a Holocaust survivor had affected my parenting and my being a grandparent. I answered that I was very protective of my children and also nervous, hoping that I was parenting the correct way. I remembered my parents' suffering and inability to protect me and my brothers during those difficult years. I must have passed on some of my insecurity to my children — I hope they are proud of my achievements and forgive me for that.

As for being a grandfather, I am extremely proud of my grandchildren. I try to give them what I can. I am sure they are affected by my experiences to some extent, and I am sure they feel some pain resulting from my life.

I feel I am one of the few privileged to have survived the Holocaust. At the same time, I feel anger toward the Nazis for being responsible for the deaths of millions of people during World War II. I am honoured to be able to tell the story of the Holocaust to students at high schools and colleges. It is the survivor's responsibility to pass on to the younger generation the stories of our families and what happened to the Jewish people.

Glossary

Aliyah Bet (Hebrew) A clandestine movement established to bring Jewish immigrants without immigration permits to British Mandate Palestine before, during and after World War II. The name, which means "ascent B," differentiates the movement from the immigrants to whom the British granted permits. Aliyah Bet organized ships to pick up Jewish immigrants from different points on the European coast in order to make the perilous journey to Palestine. Many were turned back.

antisemitism Prejudice, discrimination, persecution and/or hatred against Jewish people, institutions, culture and symbols.

Appell (German) Roll call.

Auschwitz (German; in Polish, Oświęcim) A town in southern Poland approximately forty kilometres from Krakow, it is also the name of the largest complex of Nazi concentration camps that were built nearby. The Auschwitz complex contained three main camps: Auschwitz I, a slave labour camp built in May 1940; Auschwitz II-Birkenau, a death camp built in early 1942; and Auschwitz-Monowitz, a slave labour camp built in October 1942.

In 1941, Auschwitz I was a testing site for usage of the lethal gas Zyklon B as a method of mass killing, which then went into wide usage. Between 1942 and 1944, transports arrived at Auschwitz-Birkenau from almost every country in Europe — hundreds of thousands from both Poland and Hungary, and thousands from France, the Netherlands, Greece, Slovakia, Bohemia and Moravia, Yugoslavia, Belgium, Italy and Norway. As well, more than 30,000 people were deported there from other concentration camps. It is estimated that 1.1 million people were murdered in Auschwitz; approximately 950,000 were Jewish; 74,000 Polish; 21,000 Roma; 15,000 Soviet prisoners of war; and 10,000–15,000 other nationalities. The Auschwitz complex was liberated by the Soviet army in January 1945.

bar mitzvah (Hebrew; literally, one to whom commandments apply) The time when, in Jewish tradition, children become religiously and morally responsible for their actions and are considered adults for the purpose of synagogue and other rituals. Traditionally this occurs at age thirteen for boys and twelve for girls. A bar mitzvah is also the synagogue ceremony and family celebration that mark the attainment of this status, during which the boy is called upon to read a portion of the Torah and recite the prescribed prayers in a public prayer service. During the twentieth century, liberal Jews instituted an equivalent ceremony and celebration for girls called a bat mitzvah.

Begin, Menachem (1913–1992) Israeli politician who was prime minister from 1977 to 1983. During the 1930s, Begin was a prominent member of the Zionist Betar youth movement in Poland, which led to his arrest by Soviet authorities in 1940 and his subsequent internment in a labour camp in northern Russia until 1941. Upon his release, he joined Anders' Army, and while stationed in British Mandate Palestine, he left the army in 1942 to join the Irgun — a paramilitary organization that opposed British rule in Palestine — which he commanded until 1948. During the 1960s and 1970s,

Begin led the opposition parties in Israel's parliament and became prime minister in 1977. In 1978, he and Egyptian president Anwar el-Sadat were awarded the Nobel Peace Prize for the signing of the Camp David Accords that led to a peace treaty between Egypt and Israel. *See also* Betar; British Mandate Palestine; Irgun Zvai Le'umi.

Betar A Zionist youth movement, founded by Revisionist Zionist leader Ze'ev Jabotinsky in 1923, that encouraged the development of a new generation of Zionist activists based on the ideals of courage, self-respect, military training, defence of Jewish life and property, and settlement in Israel to establish a Jewish state in British Mandate Palestine. In 1934, Betar membership in Poland numbered more than 40,000. During the 1930s and 1940s, as antisemitism increased and the Nazis launched their murderous campaign against the Jews of Europe, Betar rescued thousands of Jews by organizing illegal immigration to British Mandate Palestine. The Betar movement today, closely aligned with Israel's right-wing Likud party, remains involved in supporting Jewish and Zionist activism around the world.

B'nai Brith (Hebrew; Children of the Covenant) A volunteer-based Jewish communal agency founded in New York in 1843. Through its branches in more than fifty countries, it provides services for seniors, combats antisemitism and advocates for human rights.

British Mandate Palestine The area of the Middle East under British rule from 1923 to 1948, as established by the League of Nations after World War I. During that time, the United Kingdom severely restricted Jewish immigration. The Mandate area encompassed present-day Israel, Jordan, the West Bank and the Gaza Strip.

cholent (Yiddish) A traditional Jewish slow-cooked pot stew usually eaten as the main course at the festive Shabbat lunch on Saturdays after the synagogue service and on other Jewish holidays. For Jews of Eastern-European descent, the basic ingredients of cholent are meat, potatoes, beans and barley.

Dachau The Nazis' first concentration camp, which was established in March 1933 primarily to house political prisoners. The Dachau camp was located about sixteen kilometres northwest of Munich in southern Germany. The number of Jews interned there rose considerably after Kristallnacht pogroms on the night of November 9–10, 1938. In 1942 a crematorium area was constructed next to the main camp. By the spring of 1945, Dachau and its subcamps held more than 67,665 registered prisoners — 43,350 categorized as political prisoners and 22,100 as Jews; more than 30,000 of these prisoners were at Dachau alone. As the American Allied forces neared the camp in April 1945, the Nazis forced 7,000 prisoners, primarily Jews, on a gruelling death march to Tegernsee, another camp in southern Germany.

Displaced Persons camp Facilities set up by the Allied authorities and the United Nations Relief and Rehabilitation Administration (UNRRA) in October 1945 to resolve the refugee crisis that arose at the end of World War II. The camps provided temporary shelter and assistance to the millions of people — not only Jews — who had been displaced from their home countries as a result of the war and helped them prepare for resettlement. Approximately 30,000 Jewish DPs entered Italy between September 1946 and June 1948. Italy, which eventually set up about twenty-five DP camps to house refugees, was the main transit point for Jews to reach British Mandate Palestine. *See also* United Nations Relief and Rehabilitation Administration (UNRRA).

gefilte fish A dish generally made from chopped whitefish that is made into patties and boiled. It is traditionally eaten on Shabbat, Jewish holidays and other festive occasions.

ghetto A confined residential area for Jews. The term originated in Venice, Italy, in 1516 with a law requiring all Jews to live on a segregated, gated island known as Ghetto Nuovo. Throughout the Middle Ages in Europe, Jews were often forcibly confined to gated Jewish neighbourhoods. During the Holocaust, the Nazis forced Jews to live in crowded and unsanitary conditions in run-down districts of cities and towns. Most ghettos in Poland were enclosed by brick walls or wooden fences with barbed wire.

hanukkiyah A candelabra used during the holiday of Hanukkah. A hanukkiyah, also known as a menorah, has a place for nine candles, one of which is positioned higher or lower relative to the other eight. This candle, known as the *shamash* (Hebrew; guardian or server), is used to light the other eight candles, which represent the miracle of sanctified oil that was enough to burn for only one night yet burned for eight nights instead.

International Red Cross A humanitarian organization founded in 1863 to protect the victims of war. During World War II the Red Cross provided assistance to prisoners of war by distributing food parcels and monitoring the situation in POW camps, and also provided medical attention to wounded soldiers and civilians. Today, in addition to the international body, the International Committee of the Red Cross (ICRC), there are national Red Cross and Red Crescent societies in almost every country in the world.

Irgun Zvai Le'umi (Hebrew; National Military Organization) The Irgun (also known as the Etzel, its Hebrew acronym) was formed in 1937, after separating from the Haganah military force. Due to the increasing level of violence between Arab and Jewish citizens, the Irgun, under the leadership of Revisionist Zionist Ze'ev Jabotinsky, advocated active and armed resistance, as opposed to the policy of restraint that was advocated by the Haganah. The Irgun was also fundamental to the illegal transport and immigration of thousands of European Jews into British Mandate Palestine. The activities of the Irgun were controversial — some viewed it as a terrorist organization, while others applauded its efforts as those of freedom fighters. *See also* Jabotinsky, Ze'ev.

Jabotinsky, Vladimir Ze'ev (1880–1940) The founder of the Revisionist Zionist movement. In 1935, Jabotinsky established his own branch of nationalist Zionism, the New Zionist Organization, which advocated Jewish self-defence and self-determination. Jabotinsky strongly urged European Jews to immigrate to British Mandate Palestine and met with the governments of Hungary, Poland and Romania to advocate this "evacuation plan." He believed in establishing a Jewish state in Palestine with the support of Jewish brigades. Jabotinsky was also commander of the Irgun, the underground Jewish military organization that operated in Palestine between 1937 and 1948.

Jewish Council A group of Jewish leaders appointed by the Germans to administer and provide services to the local Jewish population under occupation and carry out Nazi orders. The Councils, which appeared to be self-governing entities but were actually under complete Nazi control, faced difficult and complex moral decisions under brutal conditions and remain a contentious subject. The chairmen had to decide whether to comply or refuse to comply with Nazi demands. Some were killed by the Nazis for refusing, while others committed suicide. Jewish officials who advocated compliance thought that cooperation might save at least some of the population. Some who denounced resistance efforts did so because they believed that armed resistance would bring death to the entire community.

kibbutz (Hebrew) A collectively owned farm or settlement in Israel, democratically governed by its members. Among some of the Zionist youth movements in Poland, the term was also used to refer to groups whose loyalty was to Palestine, although they did not yet live there. Members were organized into "kibbutz training groups" and some attended preparation training to immigrate to British Mandate Palestine. *See also* British Mandate Palestine.

Kindertransport (German; literally, children's transport) The organized attempts by British and American groups to get Jewish children out of Nazi Germany before 1939. Between December 1938 and September 3, 1939, the government-sanctioned but privately funded Kindertransport rescued nearly 10,000 children under the age of seventeen and placed them in foster homes and hostels in Britain and other safe countries.

kosher (Hebrew) Fit to eat according to Jewish dietary laws. Observant Jews follow a system of rules known as *kashruth* that regulates what can be eaten, how food is prepared and how animals and poultry are slaughtered.

Majdanek A concentration camp in Lublin, Poland, in operation from October 1941 to July 1944, when it was liberated by the Soviet army. More than 60,000 Jewish prisoners died at the camp.

March of the Living An annual event that was established in 1988 and takes place in April on Holocaust Memorial Day (Yom Ha-Shoah) in Poland. The March of the Living program aims to educate primarily Jewish students and young adults from around the world about the Holocaust and Jewish life during World War II. Along with Holocaust survivors, participants march the three kilometres from Auschwitz to Birkenau to commemorate all who perished in the Holocaust. The concept of the event comes from the Nazi death marches that Jews were forced to go on when they were being evacuated from the forced labour and concentration camps at the very end of the war. Many Jews died during these marches and the March of the Living was thus created both to remember this history and to serve as a contrast to it by celebrating Jewish life and strength. After spending time in Poland, participants travel to Israel and join in celebrations there for Israel's remembrance and independence days. *See also* Yom HaZikaron; Yom Ha'atzmaut.

matzah (Hebrew; also matza, matzoh, matzot, matsah; in Yiddish, matze) Crisp flatbread made of plain white flour and water that is not allowed to rise before or during baking. Matzah is the substitute for bread during the Jewish holiday of Passover, when eating bread and leavened products is forbidden.

minyan The quorum of ten adult male Jews required for certain religious rites. The term can also designate a congregation.

Mussolini, Benito (1883–1945) Prime minister of Italy from 1923 to 1943 and founder of the National Fascist Party. By 1925 Mussolini had adopted the title of "Il Duce" (leader), which referred to his position as both dictator and head of government. Mussolini entered into an alliance with Germany in May 1939 known as the Pact of Steel. Italy officially became part of the Axis powers in September 1940. Mussolini was ousted from government in July 1943 and executed in April 1945.

Natzweiler A town in eastern France that served as the location of a small, German-run concentration camp. About fifty subcamps — all located in France and Germany — were associated with Natzweiler, including Vaihingen. The main camp was evacuated in fall 1944, with the prisoners being sent to various subcamps. In the spring of 1945, the Germans sent the subcamp inmates on forced marches to Dachau. *See also* Vaihingen.

Orthodox Judaism The set of beliefs and practices of Jews for whom the observance of Jewish law is closely connected to faith; it is characterized by strict religious observance of Jewish dietary laws, restrictions on work on the Sabbath and holidays, and a code of modesty in dress.

Passover One of the major festivals of the Jewish calendar, Passover takes place over eight days in the spring. One of the main observances of the holiday is to recount the story of Exodus, the Jews' flight from slavery in Egypt, at a ritual meal called a seder. The name itself refers to the fact that God "passed over" the houses of the Jews when he set about slaying the firstborn sons of Egypt as the last of the ten plagues aimed at convincing Pharaoh to free the Jews.

Ravensbrück The largest Nazi concentration camp created almost exclusively for women that was established in May 1939 and located about ninety kilometres north of Berlin. Medical experiments were carried out on the women at Ravensbrück and in early 1945 the SS built a gas chamber, where approximately 5,000 to 6,000 prisoners were murdered. More than 100,000 women prisoners from all over Nazi-occupied Europe had passed through Ravensbrück before the Soviets liberated the camp on April 29–30, 1945. Approximately 50,000 women died in the camp.

Roosevelt, Franklin Delano (1882–1945) President of the United States between 1933 and 1945. Roosevelt approved military support to Britain in 1940, but the US officially entered into the war on the side of the Allies only after Japan attacked Pearl Harbor in December 1941.

Rosh Hashanah (Hebrew) New Year. The autumn holiday that marks the beginning of the Jewish year and ushers in the High Holy Days. The holiday begins with candle-lighting and a synagogue service that ends with blowing the *shofar* (ram's horn). The service is usually followed by a family dinner where sweet foods, such as apples and honey, are eaten to symbolize and celebrate a sweet new year. *See also* Yom Kippur.

SD Abbreviation for Sicherheitsdienst, the security and intelligence service of the SS. The main responsibility of the SD, which was headed by Reinhard Heydrich under the command of Heinrich Himmler, was to seek out supposed enemies of the Third Reich through huge networks of informants in the occupied territories.

Shabbat (Hebrew; in English, Sabbath; in Yiddish, Shabbes, Shabbos) The weekly day of rest beginning Friday at sunset and ending Saturday at nightfall, ushered in by the lighting of candles on Friday evening and the recitation of blessings over wine and challah (egg bread); on this day of celebration as well as prayer, it is customary to eat three festive meals, attend synagogue services and refrain from doing any work or travelling.

Sharon, Ariel (1928–2014) Officer in the Israeli army who moved into politics and served as prime minister of Israel from March 2001 to April 2006.

Shema Yisrael (Hebrew; in English, "Hear, O Israel") The first two words of a section of the Torah and an extremely important prayer in Judaism. The full verse is "Hear, O Israel: the Lord is our God, the Lord is one" and refers to faith and loyalty in one God, which is the essence of Judaism. The *Shema* prayer comprises three verses in the Torah and observant Jews recite the *Shema* daily, in the morning, evening, and at bedtime.

shtiebl (Yiddish; little house or little room) A small, unadorned prayer room or prayer house furnished more modestly than a synagogue. Most observant Jews in Eastern Europe prayed in *shtiebls* on a daily basis; they attended services in a synagogue on holidays or sometimes on Shabbat. *See also* Shabbat.

Spielberg, Steven (1946–) An American film director who founded the Survivors of the Shoah Visual History Foundation in 1994, as a result of his experience making the film *Schindler's List*. The foundation records and preserves the testimonies of Holocaust survivors in a video archive and promotes Holocaust education. In 2006, after recording almost 50,000 international testimonies, the foundation partnered with the University of Southern California and became the USC Shoah Foundation Institute for Visual History and Education.

SS (abbreviation of Schutzstaffel; Defence Corps). The SS was established in 1925 as Adolf Hitler's elite corps of personal bodyguards. Under the direction of Heinrich Himmler, its membership grew from 280 in 1929 to 50,000 when the Nazis came to power in 1933, and to nearly a quarter of a million on the eve of World War II. The SS comprised the Allgemeine-SS (General SS) and the Waffen-SS (Armed, or Combat SS). The General SS dealt with policing and the enforcement of Nazi racial policies in Germany and the Nazi-occupied countries. An important unit within the SS was the Reichssicherheitshauptamt (RSHA, the Central Office of Reich Security), whose responsibility included the Gestapo (Geheime Staatspolizei). The SS ran the concentration and death camps, with all their associated economic enterprises, and also fielded its own Waffen-SS military divisions, including some recruited from the occupied countries.

Theresienstadt (German; in Czech, Terezín) A walled town in the Czech Republic sixty kilometres north of Prague that served as both a ghetto and a concentration camp. More than 73,000 Jews from the German Protectorate of Bohemia and Moravia and from the Greater German Reich (including Austria and parts of Poland) were deported to Terezín between 1941 and 1945, 60,000 of whom were deported to Auschwitz or other death camps. Theresienstadt was liberated on May 8, 1945, by the Soviet Red Army.

Treblinka A labour and death camp created as part of Operation Reinhard, the German code word for the Nazi plan for murdering Jews in German-occupied Poland using poison gas. A slave-labour camp (Treblinka I) was built in November 1941 in the *Generalgouvernement*(General Government), near the villages of Treblinka and Małkinia Górna, about eighty kilometres northeast of Warsaw. Treblinka II, the killing centre, was constructed in 1942 in a sparsely populated and heavily wooded area about 1.5 kilometres from the labour camp and the first massive deportations there from Warsaw began on July 22, 1942. From July 1942 to October 1943 more than 750,000 Jews were killed at Treblinka, making it second to Auschwitz in the numbers of Jews killed in a Nazi camp. Treblinka I and II were both liberated by the Soviet army in July 1944.

United Nations Relief and Rehabilitation Administration (UNRRA) An international relief agency created at a 44-nation conference in Washington, DC, on November 9, 1943, to provide economic assistance and basic necessities to war refugees. It was especially active in repatriating and assisting refugees in the formerly Nazi-occupied European nations immediately after World War II.

Vaihingen A town near Stuttgart, Germany, where a forced labour camp was constructed in late 1943. There was an underground factory for manufacturing of parts for Messerschmitt airplanes; prisoners were also forced to work in nearby quarries while living on starvation rations. Vaihingen was a subcamp of the Natzweiler concentration camp, located in northeastern France near the border with Germany. *See also* Natzweiler.

Volksdeutsche The term used for ethnic Germans who lived outside Germany in Central and Eastern Europe; also refers to the ethnic German colonists who were resettled in Polish villages as part of far-reaching Nazi plans to Germanize Nazi-occupied territories in the East.

Yad Vashem The Holocaust Martyrs' and Heroes' Remembrance Authority, established in 1953 to commemorate, educate the public about, research and document the Holocaust.

yeshiva (Hebrew) A Jewish educational institution in which religious texts such as the Torah and Talmud are studied.

Yiddish A language derived from Middle High German with elements of Hebrew, Aramaic, Romance and Slavic languages, and written in Hebrew characters. Spoken by Jews in east-central Europe for roughly a thousand years from the tenth century to the mid-twentieth century, it was still the most common language among European Jews until the outbreak of World War II. There are similarities between Yiddish and contemporary German.

Yom Ha'atzmaut (Hebrew; literally, day of independence) A day marking the establishment of Israel as an independent Jewish state on May 14, 1948. Yom Ha'atzmaut is commemorated on the fifth day of the Hebrew month of Iyar and follows Yom HaZikaron, Israel's memorial day for fallen soldiers. *See also* Yom HaZikaron.

Yom HaZikaron (Hebrew; literally, day of remembrance) A day honouring Israeli soldiers who died in defense of the country, occurring on the fourth day of the Hebrew month of Iyar and preceding Yom Ha'atzmaut, Israel's Independence Day. *See also* Yom Ha'atzmaut.

Yom Kippur (Hebrew; literally, day of atonement) A solemn day of fasting and repentance that comes eight days after Rosh Hashanah, the Jewish New Year, and marks the end of the high holidays. *See also* Rosh Hashanah.

Zionism A movement promoted by the Viennese Jewish journalist Theodor Herzl, who argued in his 1896 book *Der Judenstaat* (The Jewish State) that the best way to resolve the problem of antisemitism and persecution of Jews in Europe was to create an independent Jewish state in the historic Jewish homeland of Biblical Israel. Zionists also promoted the revival of Hebrew as a Jewish national language.

Photographs

1 Amek's parents, Simon and Fay Adler (standing), with his maternal grandparents, Frida and Noah Elfenbein, and his eldest brother, Arthur. Lublin, 1919.

2 Amek's maternal grandfather, Noah Elfenbein. Lublin, circa 1910.

3 At the gravestone of Amek's maternal grandfather, Noah Elfenbein. From left to right: an unidentified cousin of Amek's maternal grandmother; Amek's maternal grandmother, Frida Elfenbein; Amek's brother Arthur; Amek's father, Simon; his mother, Fay; and Amek's brother Ben. Lublin, 1936.

1 Amek's father, Simon, and brother Joseph on holiday. Poland, 1935.
2 Amek, age 9, with his mother, Fay, on holiday. Krynica, Poland, 1937.

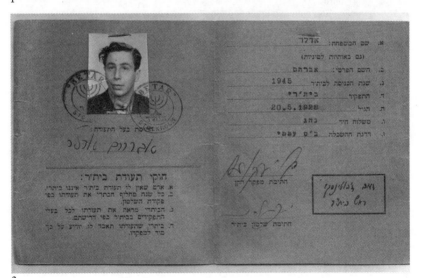

1 & 2 Amek's identity document from Betar, 1946–1947.

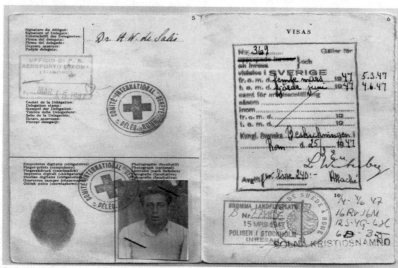

1 & 2 Amek's Red Cross passport, 1947.

1 Amek (left) with his brother Arthur. Ancona, Italy, 1946.

2 Amek. Stockholm, circa 1949.

3 Amek's brother Ben. Dachau, 1946.

4 Amek (centre) with his friends Kuba (left) and Eddie (right). Stockholm, 1949.

1 Amek with his wife, Ruth Elias, on their wedding day. Stockholm, 1950.
2 Amek and Ruth with their children, Barry and Rose. Toronto, 1960s.

Amek's mother, Fay, at a party celebrating her eightieth birthday. Toronto, 1980.

1 Amek (centre), with his brothers Arthur (left) and Ben (right). Toronto, 2001.
2 Amek's children, in-laws and grandchildren at the bat mitzvah of Amek's grand-
   daughter Staci. Back row, left to right: Amek's daughter, Rose; his son-in-law, Jeff
   Weinberg; his grandson Evan; and Amek's son, Barry. Front row, left to right:
   Amek's grandson Jordan; his granddaughter Staci; his granddaughter Megan; and
   Amek's daughter-in-law, Melissa. Toronto, 2001.

1

2

1 Amek's son's family at the joint bar and bat mitzvah of their children. From left to right: Amek's daughter-in-law, Melissa; his grandson Jordan; his granddaughter Megan; and his son, Barry. Coral Springs, Florida, 2004.

2 Amek with his family. From left to right: Amek's daughter-in-law, Melissa; his son, Barry; Amek's wife, Ruth; Amek; Amek's niece Eva Robins; her husband, Steve; Amek's daughter, Rose; and Amek's son-in-law, Jeff. Los Angeles, California, 2004.

1 Amek's daughter, Rose, with her family. From left to right: Amek's son-in-law, Jeff; Rose; Amek's granddaughter's friend, Nick; Amek's granddaughter Staci; Amek's grandson's friend, Joe; and Amek's grandson Evan. Toronto, 2012.

2 Family of Mark Adler, son of Amek's brother Arthur. From left to right: Mark's daughter's boyfriend, Adam; Mark's daughter, Maya; his wife, Susan; Mark; and his son, Ilan. Toronto, 2013.

Amek and Ruth. Detroit, 2006.

Amek, fourth from left, holding an image of the proposed monument to honour Canadian Jewish war veterans at the ground-breaking ceremony. Toronto, 2011.

Index

The Azrieli Foundation was established in 1989 to realize and extend the philanthropic vision of David J. Azrieli, C.M., C.Q., M.Arch. The Foundation's mission is to support a wide spectrum of initiatives in education and research. The Azrieli Foundation is an active supporter of programs in the fields of Education, the education of architects, scientific and medical research, and the arts. The Azrieli Foundation's many initiatives include: the Holocaust Survivor Memoirs Program, which collects, preserves, publishes and distributes the written memoirs of survivors in Canada; the Azrieli Institute for Educational Empowerment, an innovative program successfully working to keep at-risk youth in school; the Azrieli Fellows Program, which promotes academic excellence and leadership on the graduate level at Israeli universities; the Azrieli Music Project, which celebrates and fosters the creation of high-quality new Jewish orchestral music; and the Azrieli Neurodevelopmental Research Program, which supports advanced research on neurodevelopmental disorders, particularly Fragile X and Autism Spectrum Disorders.